The Little Book
of
AMERICAN
PRESIDENTS

by

PETER ELDIN, SIMON TOMLIN
and JAMIE STOKES

This is a Parragon Publishing Book
First published in 2001

Parragon Publishing
Queen Street House
4 Queen Street
Bath BA1 1HE, UK

Produced by Magpie Books, an imprint of
Constable & Robinson Publishing Ltd, London

Copyright © Parragon 2001

Cover illustration courtesy of Mary Evans Picture Library

ISBN 0-75255-917-6

A copy of the British Library Cataloguing-in-Publication Data is
available from the British Library
Printed in China

Contents

Chapter One

The Greatest

Ask the question "Who is the most famous person alive?" and the President of the United States will never be far from the number one spot. For decades the President has widely been regarded as the leader of the free world, a figurehead that symbolizes unwavering loyalty to the principles of democracy, freedom, and the rule of law. No-one – whether a politician, billionaire, or royal – has as much power and influence on the world stage.

For many, however, the enduring strength and popularity of the American presidency has in large part been thanks to a few truly great men, who set the highest example not only to their successors, but to the nation as a whole.

The broad consensus of public opinion singles out four great Presidents from the 42 men that have held the office since 1789. Two of them, George Washington and Thomas Jefferson, are founding fathers who put the nation on a firm footing and helped steer it to future greatness. The third, Abraham Lincoln – perhaps regarded as the greatest President of all – successfully led the United States through its darkest hour and secured the freedom of millions of slaves with the Emancipation Proclamation. The last of the four, and the only one from the 20th century, was the only man to be elected President four times. Franklin Delano Roosevelt both pulled the country out of the Great Depression and took the full might of the nation into World War II, instrumental in securing victory against Hitler.

This chapter will delve into the lives of these, the greatest Presidents, and examine their policies that shaped a nation.

George Washington
c.1731–99
1st President of the US (1789–97)

Notable dates

Feb 22, 1732	*Birth*
Jan 6, 1759	*Married Martha Curtis*
1775–83	*War of Independence*
June 16, 1785	*Given command of Continental Army*
Sep 17, 1787	*Signatory to Constitution of the United States*
Feb 4, 1789	*Becomes first US President*

Feb 13, 1793	Re-elected President
Mar 4, 1797	Retired from presidency
Dec 14, 1799	Death

Background

Born into a moderately wealthy land-owning family at Pope's Creek plantation in the then British colony of Virginia, George Washington's early life was comfortable but marred by tragedy. Washington's father died when George was 14 years old and he went to live with his older half-brother, Lawrence, who had married into the very wealthy Fairfax family.

By the age of 16, Washington was learning the skills of surveying in the wild new lands of North Virginia. Just four years later, Lawrence was dead, as was his one surviving child, and the Mount Vernon estate passed to Washington. Barely 20, he found himself master of a well-appointed estate that was to become a beloved home for the rest of his life.

French and Indian Wars

From 1753 to 1759, Washington served in the Virginia militia in campaigns against French incursions into British-claimed territory. By the age of 23, he had risen through the ranks to become commander-in-chief of Virginia's armed forces.

With victory achieved, Washington resigned his commission and returned to Mount Vernon. He soon married a wealthy young widow, Martha Curtis. Although their union was childless, it was happy and long, and Washington cared for her two children as if they were his own.

Washington made himself busy with the duties of his estate and would no doubt, if circumstances had not been different, settled down to a quiet and civilized life. Unfortunately, trouble was brewing.

Background to the American Revolution

British success in the French and Indian Wars gave them control of all lands from the Atlantic to the Mississippi. The British government now began to insist that the American colonists should pay for the protection of Britain's armed forces via increased taxation.

Like many other Virginians, Washington felt that

it was morally unacceptable for the British government to demand taxation of the American colonists without allowing them representation in Parliament. The stresses that were to lead to a revolution built up rapidly. Protests, such as the Boston Tea Party, began to flare up as signals that rebellion was on the way.

Washington was in no way a radical. He disliked the idea of revolution and was described by those who knew him as a modest, sensible man, slow to take action. Despite this, he was a man who felt compelled to act in defense of right, even if it meant complicating his beloved home life.

Revolution

In the fall of 1774, Washington was elected as one of seven delegates in Virginia to attend the First Continental Congress – a meeting of all 13 colonies at Philadelphia. His good sense and clear-headedness when others were demanding hasty action earned him respect.

Spring of the following year saw Washington again representing Virginia at the Second Continental Congress. The first skirmishes between British troops and colonists had already taken place and Boston was under martial law. When the call came for Pennsylvania, Maryland, and Virginia to send troops to aid Boston, a decision was taken to elect a commander-in-chief for the colonial army. On June 15, 1775, George Washington was unanimously elected to the post. His one condition for taking on the job was that he should be paid no salary.

As a military commander, Washington was never brilliant and he never commanded a force that was capable of defeating the well-trained, well-equipped British army in open battle. Despite the tremendous difficulty of the task, Washington never lost sight of what he was fighting for and never gave in to the temptations of personal ambition.

The war dragged on for eight bitter years. Washington believed that the only realistic strategy was to simply keep fighting until the British were fed up with the cost of keeping their army fed and equipped and simply left the field. He was proved correct, but only after hardships that must have made him long for the comforts of Mount Vernon.

Washington's army rarely numbered more than 10,000 men and was often half that. They lacked ammunition, basic supplies, even boots, and Washington had to battle constantly to get Congress to pay his soldiers' wages. Only Washington's ability to inspire the loyalty of his men kept the army together and only Washington's grim determination to keep fighting persuaded the British they could never win.

It wasn't until December of 1783 that Washington was finally able to resign and return to his neglected Mount Vernon estates. He was 51 years old and physically and mentally exhausted, yet the greatest achievements of his life still lay in the future.

Presidential record

Washington was not an intellectually brilliant man. He disliked debates and shied away from philosophical argument, but he was a great national leader revered almost as highly in his own time as he is today.

As President, he guided the United States through the time of its greatest vulnerability – its infancy. His characteristic caution and moderation became the model for the American vision of the ideal president. In Washington, the American people found a father figure, a man committed to serving the good of the people and a man the people felt that they could trust implicitly.

Election

With the war won, the mission that had held the colonists together as a united group disappeared. Quickly the states began to grow apart as local rivalries and ambitions took effect. It was clear that this new nation needed a constitution to bind it together.

As the only man universally acclaimed and respected in all the 13 states, it was inevitable that George Washington would be called upon to preside over the Constitutional Convention held in Philadelphia in 1787.

Once the constitution was drawn up, which provided for a president of the United States to be elected by an electoral college, there was little doubt as to who that man would be. In April of 1789, at the age of 57, George Washington became the first President of the United States with a unanimous vote. It was Washington's preference that he and future holders of his office should be addressed simply as "Mr President."

In office Washington saw his duty as maintaining the strict segregation of the executive, legislative, and judicial branches of government, of administrating the laws of Congress, and of managing foreign affairs.

Above all, he saw it as his duty to establish the office of the presidency as an office to be trusted and respected by all Americans. His personal qualities insured that he succeeded in that goal better than anybody else could have and in so doing handed the United States a legacy of stable and accountable government.

Second term

When Washington was re-elected President in 1792, his greatest concern was the power struggle between Thomas Jefferson and Alexander Hamilton. Out of this conflict arose the first political parties, a development that Washington regarded with suspicion, although he knew that he could do little to stop it.

Within a year, a major war broke out in Europe as several nations allied themselves against what was to become Napoleonic France. Jefferson and others were calling for the United States to go to France's aid but Washington was wary.

Although a treaty existed between the United States and France, and although France had aided the Americans in their revolution, Washington felt that his young nation was still too fragile to take on a major conflict. In April of 1793, he issued the Neutrality Proclamation which made it clear that the United

States wasn't going to offer its help to any of the warring states. This act set a precedent that was to inform US foreign policy until the outbreak of the World War I more than a century later.

Retirement

As he neared the end of his second term in office, Washington began to look forward to a long and happy retirement secure in the knowledge that his lifetime of service had won peace and prosperity for his nation. In his farewell address he wrote, "Observe good faith and justice towards all nations; cultivate peace and harmony with all."

Sadly, the great man's long-deserved retirement was to prove short lived. On the evening of December 13, 1799, Washington was taken ill at his Mount Vernon home. All through the following day his condition worsened and that night he died. He had been out of office for only a year.

Thomas Jefferson

1743–1826
3rd President of the US (1801–09)
Democratic-Republican

Notable dates

Apr 13, 1743	*Birth*
Jan 1, 1772	*Married Martha Skelton*
1775–83	*War of Independence*
July 4, 1776	*Declaration of Independence*
Mar 22, 1790	*Becomes first US Secretary of State*
Feb 8, 1707	*Elected Vice-President*
Feb 17, 1801	*Elected President*

Feb 13, 1805	Re-elected President
Mar 4, 1809	Retired from presidency
July 4, 1826	Death

Background

Thomas Jefferson was born into a wealthy, land-owning family in the then British colony of Virginia. At the age of 14, on the death of his father, he inherited the family estate, known as Shadwell.

Jefferson studied for two years at William and Mary College in Williamsburg but did not take a degree. Immediately, he went to work at a law office and began studying to become a lawyer. In 1767, at the age of 24, he was admitted to the Virginia Bar. By this time he was already a Justice of the Peace.

Jefferson was an exceptionally brilliant man and it was almost inevitable that he would be persuaded to enter politics. In 1769, he was elected to the Virginia House of Burgesses and was subsequently re-elected every year until 1775.

Marriage to a young widow, Mrs Martha Skelton, followed two years after the Jefferson family home, Shadwell, was destroyed by fire in 1770. Jefferson built a mansion to his own design in Monticello which was to become his home for the rest of his life.

Little is known about Jefferson's wife. She died at the age of 33 after they had been married for nearly 10 years. Of the five children she had with Jefferson, only two daughters survived into adulthood. Rumours later circulated that Jefferson began an affair with an African American nursemaid named Sally Hemmings, but little evidence has ever been presented.

Revolution and Independence

By 1774, the revolution that was to create the United States of America was fast approaching. Rebellions, skirmishes, and riots were breaking out throughout the 13 colonies and Jefferson, like many of his class, felt strongly that open revolt against British rule was necessary and desirable.

Jefferson was a philosophical man and was outraged by what he saw as immoral government by the British. He was also a man of vision and quick wits who saw an opportunity to create a new kind of nation out of the 13 colonies.

In 1775, he was elected as a delegate for Virginia to the Second Continental Congress – a meeting of representatives from all 13 colonies. By the time the congress convened, the first skirmishes of the revolutionary war had already taken place. George Washington was elected to command the colonial army and the long struggle for independence began.

Declaration of Independence

By the spring of 1776, the British had failed to respond to demands for fairer government and the colonists' resolve to break free entirely had hardened. Jefferson was elected to a five-man committee tasked with the drafting of a declaration of independence.

Jefferson wrote the draft and it was approved by Congress with only minor changes on July 4. It was to prove one of the most influential documents in history.

Jefferson's Declaration of Independence summed up the new ideals of social and political justice that had been introduced by philosophers such as John Locke and Thomas Paine. It clearly and eloquently stated the colonists' reasons for rebellion – that people have the right to overthrow an unjust government. It set out other basic human rights: "We hold these truths to be self-evident, that all men are created equal, that they are endowed by their creator with certain unalienable rights, that among these are life, liberty, and the pursuit of happiness."

Vice-President

From 1784 to 1789, Jefferson represented Congress as an envoy to France. On his return he was persuaded to join George Washington's government as Secretary of State. During this period he became a sharp critic of Washington and his disputes with Secretary of the Treasury, Alexander Hamilton, saw the emergence of the first political parties in US politics.

Following George Washington's resignation, Jefferson stood as the Democratic-Republican candidate and was elected Vice-President under the Federalist John Adams.

Presidential record

Most historians agree that Thomas Jefferson is the most brilliant and talented man ever to have occupied the office of the President of the United States.

During the course of his presidency he shrewdly managed a deal that doubled the size of the United

States and ensured that expansion right across the continent would be possible. In office he worked tirelessly to ensure that the freedoms won in revolution would not be lost as the young nation developed.

First term
The great triumph of Jefferson's first term was the Louisiana Purchase. A vast tract of land stretching from the Mississippi to the Rocky Mountains had originally been claimed by France, ceded to Spain, and then handed back to France again in 1801.

When Jefferson heard that Napoleon, then Emperor of France, was intending to send colonists to this unsettled region, he sent representatives to France to discuss the matter. He could foresee that colonization would forever limit the United States to the Eastern seaboard.

Amazingly, a deal was struck and France agreed to hand over the territories to the United States for a fee of 11,250,000 US dollars. Overnight the size of the United States was doubled. When settlers began moving into the new territories, they discovered fertile agricultural lands worth immeasurably more than Jefferson had paid for them.

Second term

The election of 1804 saw Jefferson returned for a second term with a huge majority of the electoral college vote. Two years later, Jefferson's grandson, James Madison Randolph, became the first child to be born in the White House.

Foreign affairs proved to be Jefferson's biggest headache during his second term. In 1803, Britain and France had gone to war and Jefferson faced a similar problem to that Washington had faced – how to avoid being drawn into a conflict that could bring no benefit to the United States.

Jefferson believed that he could keep the United States out of the fight and bring the warring nations to the peace table by shutting off American supplies. A law was forced through Congress banning exports to Britain or France and US ships were forbidden from entering foreign ports.

In fact, the measures proved far more harmful to the United States than to either Britain or France and the bill was repealed two years later.

Retirement

Thomas Jefferson enjoyed a long and productive retirement after he left the White House in 1809. He studied and made significant contributions to the fields of chemistry, education, law, philosophy, and music.

One of his proudest achievements was his founding of the University of Virginia in 1825. He not only designed the buildings, he devised the curriculum and chose the staff as well. Jefferson's extensive library was purchased by Congress and formed the core of the new Library of Congress.

Despite the sale of his library, Jefferson was in constant financial trouble – his hospitality and generosity cost him dearly. A gift of several thousand dollars was all that saved him from bankruptcy and the loss of his house in the final year of his life.

Abraham Lincoln

1809–65
16th President of the US (1861–65)
Republican

Notable dates

Feb 12, 1809	*Birth*
Nov 4, 1842	*Married Mary Ann Todd*
Mar 4, 1861	*Presidential oath of office*
1861–65	*Civil War*
Sep 22, 1862	*Emancipation Proclamation*

Jan 1, 1863	*Final Emancipation Proclamation*
Jan 31, 1865	*Re-elected President*
Apr 14, 1865	*Shot by assassin*
Apr 15, 1865	*Death*

Background

Born in a log cabin in the hard frontier lands of Kentucky, Abraham Lincoln's early years were characterized by hardship, poverty, and instability. The family was almost constantly on the move, following the relentless drive west in search of prosperity.

Schooling was hard to come by and the future President spent barely a year in formal education. Leaving home at the age of 21 Lincoln took on a series of temporary jobs in and around the small town of New Salem, Illinois.

Voracious reading during his early twenties helped Lincoln make up for his lack of formal education. During this period he became interested in politics and was urged by friends to stand for election to the state legislature. In 1834, he was elected and went on to serve for eight years in the lower house of the Illinois General Assembly.

1834 was also the year that Lincoln began to study law. He would walk the 20 miles to a lawyer friend's home to borrow books. After four years, his hard work paid off when he received a license to practice. It was the beginning of a highly successful legal career.

By now Lincoln was married to Mary Todd. Their relationship suffered considerable strain from her obsessive personality. It was said that the great man was forced to carry numerous pairs of his wife's gloves stuffed into every pocket so that she could change them whenever she spied a spot of dirt on one.

Presidential record

Lincoln became President on the eve of the greatest crisis the United States had ever faced – the Civil War. Partly by good fortune but largely by political skill, Lincoln won a war and laid the foundation for the modern superpower that the United States has become.

Background to the War

In 1846, Lincoln was elected to Congress. He spent two undistinguished years earning a reputation as a troublemaker before returning to Springfield to concentrate on his legal practice. It would be almost a five years before he returned to the political fray.

During this period pressures that had been building up in the United States for a quarter of a century started to reach a crisis point. US politics had been dominated by the Democratic Party which was itself dominated by wealthy and sophisticated Southerners. But things were changing rapidly in the North. The drive west, massive immigration, and accelerating industrialization meant that the North had become more populous, more productive, and more wealthy. Furthermore, the economy of the North was not based on slavery and there was considerable moral opposition to the institution.

The Slave Issue

Slavery was the issue that brought Lincoln back into politics. In 1854, the Kansas-Nebraska bill was presented. If passed it would mean that the new western states would be able to decide for themselves whether slavery was to be legal there or not.

Lincoln brilliantly opposed the bill in a series of public debates, but it still became law. Lincoln did not at this point believe that slavery should be abolished in the South; he believed it would die out of its own accord, but he was opposed to the institution being extended to the new states of the West.

Lincoln decided to join the newly formed Republican party. Dominated by Northerners, the Republicans included a large body of fanatical abolitionists.

Election

In 1856, the South won a temporary victory when the Democrat Buchanan was elected to the White House. In practice it only served to raise tensions. Three years later, Lincoln was selected as the Republicans' presidential candidate.

When the results were declared and it became clear that Lincoln had won the presidency, it also became clear that not a single Southern or border state had voted for him.

In the period between Lincoln's election in November and his inauguration the following March, the Union was wrenched in two. Led by South Carolina, 11 Southern states declared their secession from the Union and formed the Confederate States of America. War was inevitable.

The Civil War

"If there be those who would not save the Union less they could destroy slavery, I do not agree with them. My paramount object in this struggle is to save the Union..."

These words make clear Lincoln's priorities in the war that dominated his time in office. The first great battle of the conflict, the First Battle of Bull Run, took place on July 21, 1861. Evenly matched Union and Confederate armies faced each other across the Potomac and when Union forces pushed forward they were soundly defeated. It became clear to the North that the war was going to be long and hard.

Lincoln realized that if the Union states bordering the Confederacy were to switch sides then the Union could be facing defeat. Support for abolitionism was practically non-existent in these states, forcing Lincoln to play down the abolitionist hopes of his own party and many in the North.

In the early stages of the conflict Lincoln took on almost dictatorial powers. He expanded the size of the army beyond the limits set by law, suspended the writ of *habeas corpus*, and ordered the spending of Federal funds without the approval of Congress. Later, he justified these measures as necessary for the protection of the Union and allowed under the President's special war powers set out in the Constitution.

Emancipation Proclamation

Slowly the economic strength of the North began to tell in the war. Public opinion was also coming around to the idea that ending slavery was a valid war aim and Lincoln decided that a change in policy could be made.

Following a Union victory at the Battle of Antietam in September 1862, Lincoln issued his Emancipation Proclamation. In it he stated that all slaves in the rebel (Confederate) states "are, and hence-foreward shall be, free." In practice the proclamation did not free a single slave since it applied only to Confederate territories, but it made a policy statement that would later be upheld with the passing of the 13th amendment banning slavery in the United States.

Gettysburg Address

Union armies won two significant victories in 1863, at Gettysburg and Vicksburg. On November 19 of that year, Lincoln attended ceremonies to dedicate a cemetery on the Gettysburg battlefield and made a short speech that has become one of the best-loved and often quoted political statements in US history:

"Four score and seven years ago our fathers brought forth to this Continent a new nation, conceived in liberty and dedicated to the proposition that all men are created equal . . . It was for us, the living, rather to be dedicated here to the great task remaining before us – that from these honored dead we take increased devotion to that cause to which they gave the last full measure of devotion; that we here resolve that these dead shall not have died in vain; that this nation, under God, was for a new birth of freedom; and that government of the people, by the people, for the people, shall not perish from the Earth."

Second term

In 1864, with the war almost won, Republicans and Democrats who supported Lincoln's war aims formed the National Union Party. Lincoln was selected as their presidential candidate and duly elected by a massive majority of electoral votes.

When Lincoln took the oath of office for a second term on March 4, 1865, the war had only a month left to run. General Lee's surrender on April 9 was met by Lincoln's generous terms of surrender.

Louisiana quickly applied for re-admission to the Union and Lincoln accepted, brushing aside the demands of those who wanted a harsher settlement to be forced on the rebel states. In his last public address, Lincoln said of the seceded states "finding themselves safely at home, it would be utterly immaterial whether they had ever been abroad."

It was a moment of great personal and political triumph for Lincoln. He had saved the Union and laid the foundation for an end to slavery. He had just four days left to live.

Assassination

On the evening of April 14, 1865, Lincoln and his wife attended a performance of the comedy *Our American Cousin* at Ford's Theater in Washington.

Shortly after 10 o'clock, the actor and Southern sympathizer John Wilkes Booth shot Lincoln in the head from the rear of the presidential box. Leaping from the box to the stage Booth brandished a dagger and cried "*Sic temper tyrranis*" (thus always to tyrants). Despite breaking his leg on landing, Booth escaped.

The mortally wounded President was taken to a nearby house where he died at 7.22 pm the next day. Booth made his way to Virginia where, after refusing to surrender, he was killed by Federal troops.

The tragically futile end to Lincoln's life added the final touch to a story that generations of Americans would come to see as the embodiment of public service, moral sense, and political decency.

Franklin Delano Roosevelt

1882–1945
32nd President of the US (1933–45)
Democrat

Notable dates

Jan 30, 1882	*Birth*
Mar 17, 1905	*Married Eleanor Roosevelt*
1914–18	*World War I*
1929–32	*Governor of New York*
Nov 8, 1932	*Elected President*
Nov 3, 1936	*Re-elected President*
1939–45	*World War II*
Nov 5, 1940	*Re-elected President*

Dec 7, 1941	*Japanese attack Pearl Harbor – US enters war*
Nov 7, 1944	*Re-elected*
Apr 12, 1945	*Death*

Background

Franklin Delano Roosevelt was born into a life of high status and enormous privilege. His father was the Vice-President of a railroad company and owner of the Springwood Estate in New York.

Roosevelt was educated at Harvard, where he studied History, and then entered the Columbia University Law School. Passing the bar examination at the age of 25, he started work for a New York City law firm but never showed any enthusiasm or real talent for legal work.

When, in 1905, Roosevelt married his distant cousin, Anne Eleanor Roosevelt, one of the most powerful partnerships in US political history was formed. Eleanor Roosevelt was to become almost as well-known and universally respected as her husband. She worked hard for underprivileged groups and supported her husband when illness almost cost him his political career.

In 1910, the future President was elected to the New York Senate and began his long and outstanding political career. When the United States entered World War I in 1917, Roosevelt had risen to the position of Assistant Secretary of the navy. The end of the war saw him touring European battlefields and meeting with war leaders. He soon became a well-recognized and well-liked public figure.

At his summer home near New Brunswick, Canada, in 1921, Roosevelt fell victim to a severe case of polio myelitis. For a time he lost the use of his legs and hands and it seemed that his career was over. Slowly, and with great encouragement from Eleanor, Roosevelt fought back against the disease.

By 1924, he was again active in politics. His appearance at the Democratic National Convention was greeted with cheers and thunderous applause in recognition of his bravery. Although he regained the use of his hands and was able to stand, he was never again able to walk without leg braces and then only for short distances.

Presidential record

First term

When the election of 1932 came around, Roosevelt had already won the governorship of New York and been re-elected to that office by the largest majority the state had ever seen.

The Great Depression was then bringing ever increasing misery and economic ruin to the nation and Roosevelt fought a campaign that promised help for the average American — the "forgotten man" as Roosevelt termed him. Securing the nomination of the Democratic Party, he went on to win a large majority of the electoral votes against the incumbent Republican President Hoover.

On March 9, 1933, directed by Roosevelt, Congress began a special session that became known as the "100 Days." During this period Roosevelt set about creating laws to help the nation recover from the economic crisis — almost all of which were passed by Congress. On March 12, he made a radio broadcast to the nation in which he explained what had to be done. These "fireside chats" were to become a regular feature of his time in office and served to build a bond of trust between Roosevelt and the American people.

Roosevelt's reform programme became known as

the New Deal. His aim was to reduce unemployment through state-sponsored work projects and to pump government money into the economy to get industry back on its feet. Some criticized the "useless" work done by people on these projects, but they helped save millions from absolute poverty.

In foreign policy Roosevelt pursued what he called the "good neighbor policy." This included recognizing the Communist government of the Soviet Union and re-establishing diplomatic and trade links for the first time since 1917.

Second term

An overwhelming majority of the electoral college vote brought Roosevelt back to the Oval Office in 1936. He won all the states except two. Once in office, Japanese aggression against China became his greatest preoccupation. He refused to recognize the puppet state that the Japanese had set up in China and tried to enlarge the armed forces – although Congress opposed him in this.

Throughout this period Congress passed a series of Neutrality Acts designed to prevent the United States from becoming involved in foreign wars. These acts fairly reflected the views of many Americans but they made Roosevelt uneasy and he constantly pushed for greater flexibility in attitudes toward US foreign policy.

When World War II began in September, 1939, a majority of Americans were steadfastly opposed to any involvement. Privately Roosevelt felt that if Germany, Italy, and Japan were to be victorious, then democracy would be threatened all over the world – including in the United States.

Third term

When the Democratic Party nominated Roosevelt as its presidential candidate for the third time, it was an unprecedented move in the history of the United States and has never been repeated since. Roosevelt continued to insist that he would keep the nation out of the war and continue his programme of recovery.

The electorate, realizing that the country needed a proven and experienced man during this period of global crisis, re-elected Roosevelt with a large majority. Largely through Roosevelt's efforts the attitude of Congress had softened towards trading with nations at war by this time. An agreement was reached allowing the British government to "purchase" 50 warships in exchange for long leases on naval bases in the Atlantic.

January 1941 saw Roosevelt making a speech that was to shift American policy. The President declared that all peoples were entitled to freedom of speech, freedom of worship, freedom from want, and freedom from fear. It was a sign that Roosevelt intended to make a stand against the repressive regime that Nazi Germany was imposing on Europe.

By December, agreements had been reached allowing war supplies to be sent to any nation at war that the President deemed vital to national security. American-made equipment began pouring into Britain, which was then fighting for its life against German aggression.

December 7, 1941 – "a date that will live in infamy" – the day that Japanese forces launched an unprovoked and devastating attack on the US Naval base at Pearl Harbor, Hawaii. Within days the United States was at war with all three axis powers – Germany, Italy, and Japan.

After conferences with British premier, Winston Churchill, and the Soviet leader, Stalin, Roosevelt decided that the weight of the United States' forces must first be brought to bear against Germany. Plans were laid that ultimately lead to the allied invasion of Europe and the defeat of Nazi Germany.

Fourth term

Just as his third had been, Roosevelt's fourth nomination and election as President was unprecedented and has never been repeated. Roosevelt himself was in poor health when he began his last term in office. Even for a man with his reserves of physical and mental strength overseeing the war effort was a huge strain.

Two days after his inauguration, Roosevelt was with Churchill and Stalin at Yalta, a resort in the Soviet Union on the Black Sea. The conference that these three leaders held shaped the history of Europe after the war. Plans for the final assault on Germany were made, and for its occupation after the war. The foundations of the United Nations were also laid. It was to be Roosevelt's last significant act.

Two months later, while Roosevelt was resting at a favorite spring resort that soothed his polio symptoms, he suffered a cerebral haemorrhage. Within hours the great man was dead. He did not live to see his nation's final victory over Japan, or to see his warnings about the Soviet Union's attitude to Europe justified.

Chapter Two

True Americans

I F THE FIRST CHAPTER dealt with "The Greatest," then this chapter deals with those Presidents who, through their actions, policies, or downright stubbornness, have earned the respect of the American people. Three of the four Presidents detailed in the first chapter have become immortalized on Mount Rushmore. The fourth head to appear on that monument, Theodore Roosevelt, belongs in this chapter, though many of the other Presidents contained within this chapter might well have staked a claim to this honor. Some of them, like the hot-headed Andrew Jackson, had they been alive when it was carved, might well have demanded that they took their place alongside the greats!

Though not all of these Presidents were popular during their terms of office, these True Americans have stood the test of time. History and the benefit of hindsight has put their actions into perspective, and most Americans would agree that the following Presidents guided America with integrity and decency, standing up for and defending their beliefs for the good of the nation.

These men have guided America through torrid times, from the War of 1812 against the might of the British armies, through two World Wars, to the more sinister Cold War, where the destruction of the entire planet was at stake. Their policies and strength of character helped to put America on the right road for economic and diplomatic success, and each of them in some measure shaped the nation into the world power that it has become today.

John Adams

1735–1826
2nd President of the US (1797–1801)
Federalist

Notable dates

Oct 30, 1735	*Birth*
Oct 25, 1764	*Married Abigail Smith*
1775–83	*War of Independence*
Apr 21, 1789	*Elected Vice-President*
Mar 4, 1793	*Second term as Vice-President*
Mar 4, 1797	*Presidential oath of office*
Mar 4, 1801	*Retired from presidency*
July 4, 1826	*Death*

Background

John Adams was born on October 30, 1735, on a small farm in Braintree (now Quincy), Massachusetts. Though his parents were not educated, John attended local schools and had private tuition, and went on to graduate from Harvard in 1755. After a short period as a teacher, he studied law, and on November 6, 1758, was admitted to the Massachusetts Bar in Boston, where he became a leading attorney.

On October 25, 1764, Adams married Abigail Smith, his third cousin, who, aged 19, was nine years his junior. They had five children, and their eldest son, John Quincy Adams, became the 6th President of the United States.

Adams took a leading role in opposing British colonial policies in America. In 1765, the British passed the Stamp Act, which taxed newspapers, and other items in America. Adams was furious and wrote resolutions against the tax, arguing that it was illegal because the people had not consented to it. In 1766, the Act was repealed.

The British tax on tea enraged Adams, and when a band of patriots dumped large quantities of it into Boston Harbor (the "Boston Tea Party"), he declared it "the most magnificent movement of all."

Although fiercely opposed to the British, Adams was led foremost by a sense of justice. When a group of British soldiers opened fire on a crowd in Boston (the "Boston Massacre"), it was Adams who represented them in court.

From 1774–78, Adams was a member of the Continental Congress, and insisted that the colonies should be independent. He persuaded Congress to create the Continental Army, led by George Washington. He was also appointed to the committee to write the Declaration of Independence. During the War of Independence, Adams' role was as peace mediator, and he was one of the men who drew up the final peace treaty with Britain.

Presidential record

In 1789, when George Washington was elected President, Adams became the first Vice-President, a role which he described as "the most insignificant office that ever the invention of man contrived or his imagination conceived." When Washington refused to serve a third term, Adams was elected President, with Thomas Jefferson as his Vice-President.

The Federalist Split

During Adams' term of office, the government faced many domestic difficulties and European relations remained hostile. Adams' own party became split over foreign policy, and two parties emerged: the Federalists, who believed that government should be ruled by a select elite, and the Republicans, who believed the system should be run by the masses. Adams was elected by the Federalists.

Conflict with France

In the wars following the French Revolution, European warships attacked American ships, with both the British and French claiming the right to seize American vessels. Adams commissioned the first US Navy, but remained committed to peace. His own party was split – some wished for peace, others wanted war with France. The Alien and Sedition Acts of 1798 were set up to quell criticism of the Federalists, making it a crime to criticize the government, President or Congress. Many believed the Acts violated freedom of speech, and they proved immensely unpopular.

Adams never used the Acts, and in 1800, secured a peace treaty with France, but he lost the election of 1800 to Jefferson, largely because of ill-feeling toward the legislation.

Retirement
Adams lived to see his son elected President. In an incredible coincidence, Jefferson and Adams died on the same day, July 4, 1826, 50 years to the day after the Declaration of Independence was signed. He was 90 when he passed away.

James Madison

1751–1836
4th President of the US (1809–17)
Republican

Notable dates

Mar 16, 1751	*Birth*
Sep 15, 1794	*Married Dorothea Payne Todd*
Mar 4, 1809	*Presidential oath of office*
June 19, 1812	*War declared against Britain*
Mar 4, 1813	*2nd presidential oath of office*
Dec 24, 1814	*Treaty of Ghent signed*
Feb 17, 1815	*Official end of the War of 1812*

Mar 4, 1817   *Retired from presidency*
June 28, 1836   *Death*

Background

James Madison was born on March 16, 1751, the eldest of ten surviving children, at Port Conway, King George County, Virginia. He was recognized as a brilliant scholar, and graduated in 1771 from the College of New Jersey (later Princeton University), where he showed interest in government and the law. He stayed on until April the following year to study Hebrew and ethics.

Madison soon became immersed in politics. In 1776, he was a member of the Virginian Convention, and he served in the Continental Congress (1780–83, 1787). He won great admiration for his role in the Constitutional Convention of 1787, where his political skill and ability to engineer compromises won him the title "Father of the Constitution."

In 1788, Madison played an instrumental part at the Virginia Convention. He led the campaign in support of Virginia's ratification of the Constitution, ensuring that the state became the tenth to ratify. In Congress, he helped frame and ensure passage of the Bill of Rights.

Madison committed himself to politics, and as a result remained a bachelor until he was 43. On September 15, 1794, he married Mrs Dorothea Payne Todd, a widow aged just 26. This proved to be a very successful partnership. Madison was thought of as shy in the social scene, but "Dolly" was loved for her warmth and gaiety. During his presidency, Dolly became the toast of Washington.

He returned to politics because of his outrage over the Alien and Sedition Acts of 1798, which made it a crime to criticize the Federalist government. In 1801, he was made Secretary of State by President Jefferson. Together, they fought bitterly against the Acts.

Presidential record

In 1809, Madison succeeded Jefferson as President, and like his predecessor, immediately became enmeshed in European wars and the consequential damage done to US commerce. Diplomacy failed to prevent the seizure of US ships, and the country entered a depression.

The War of 1812

Madison applied diplomatic techniques and economic sanctions which were effective against France, but war with Britain seemed inevitable. On June 19, 1812, the US officially declared war against Britain. Madison launched a series of attacks against Canada, Britain's most vulnerable target. Poorly trained troops and generals and internal political wrangling made the war extremely difficult.

In December, 1814, Madison and his cabinet fled to Virginia when the Executive Mansion, the Capitol, and almost all other government offices were burned by the British in retaliation for the attacks on Canada. During restoration, the Executive Mansion was painted white, gaining the name the White House, though this title only became official under Theodore Roosevelt in 1901.

The Treaty of Ghent was negotiated in December 1814. The Treaty, which established peace on the basis of the pre-war relationship with Great Britain, might have been viewed as a failure. The Americans would have gained nothing from the war, but for the fact that news of the Treaty failed to reach Washington until February 17, 1815. In the meantime, future President Andrew Jackson scored a spectacular victory over the British at the Battle of New Orleans, and most Americans believed that they had won the war.

After the war

American independence had survived the war, and Madison's final years as President were concurrent with a strong feeling of nationalism and pride for the nation. Madison retired from office on March 4, 1817.

During his later years, Madison was active in the American Colonization Society, whose mission was the resettlement of slaves in Africa. This was despite the fact that he had been a slaveholder all his life.

James Monroe

1758–1831
5th President of the US (1817–25)
Democratic-Republican

Notable dates

Apr 28, 1758   *Born*
1775–83   *War of Independence*
Feb 16, 1786   *Married Elizabeth Kortright*
1812–15   *War of 1812*
Dec 4, 1816   *Presidential oath of office*
Dec 6, 1820   *2nd presidential oath of office*
Mar 4, 1825   *Retired from presidency*
July 4, 1831   *Death*

Background

James Monroe was born in Westmoreland County, Virginia, on April 28, 1758. His education was cut short when he decided to join the army to fight in the American Revolution. In 1778, he was sent to raise troops in Virginia. He failed in this mission, but came into contact with Thomas Jefferson, who was the Governor of the state at the time.

Monroe began to study law under Jefferson. He was elected to the assembly of Virginia in 1782, and to the Congress of the Confederation in the following year. In 1786, he settled down to practice law in Fredericksburg, but was soon drawn back into politics.

On February 16, 1786, Monroe married 17-year-old Elizabeth Kortright. The couple had two daughters and one son, but the boy died as an infant.

He became a Senator in 1790, and joined with James Madison and Thomas Jefferson to oppose the Federalists. The three of them founded the Democratic-Republican party.

In 1803, Thomas Jefferson (then President) sent Monroe to Paris to help negotiate the purchase of New Orleans from the French, which succeeded. In fact, the French agreed to sell the entire Louisiana Territory. Jefferson's confidence in Monroe grew, and he appointed him as minister to Britain.

When he returned from Britain in 1807, he became a reluctant candidate for President, but lost the nomination and the presidency to James Madison. Madison appointed Monroe as his Secretary of State in 1811, at a time when relations with Britain and France were tense.

War broke out in 1812 against Britain, and Monroe was appointed Secretary of War in 1814, while still Secretary of State. His popularity grew when the American armies won several victories, and the electorate spoke when, on December 4, 1816, he was elected President by 183 electoral votes to 34.

Presidential record

Monroe's administration was a time of peaceful prosperity for America, and became known as the "era of good feeling." After the 1816 election, the Federalist Party all but disappeared, and most people supported the Democratic-Republicans. The country prospered because of the settlement of the West and fast-growing industries.

Diplomacy

Monroe's years as President marked one of the most brilliant periods in American diplomacy. He oversaw the acquisition of Florida from the Spanish. In 1817, he signed the Rush-Bagot Agreement with the British, limiting British naval forces in the Great Lakes region.

Following his re-election (in which he won all but one of the electoral votes), most of the Spanish-owned colonies in South America declared independence from Spain. In December, 1823, Monroe proclaimed the Monroe Doctrine in a message to Congress, a doctrine which has remained a basic American policy ever since. The doctrine embodied the principle that the American continents were "henceforth not to be considered as subjects for future colonization by any European powers."

Monroe retired from the presidency on March 4, 1825, and found his finances in dire straits. The salary of the President was fixed at 25,000 US dollars a year in 1789, and was not increased until 1873, when it was doubled. He appealed to Congress to pay him back for expenses, eventually receiving 30,000 US dollars in 1831. He died on Independence Day of the same year.

John Quincy Adams

1767–1848
6th President of the US (1825–29)
Republican

Notable dates

July 11, 1767	*Birth*
July 26, 1797	*Married Louisa Catherine Johnson*
Mar 4, 1825	*Presidential oath of office*
Mar 4, 1829	*Retired from presidency*
Feb 23, 1848	*Death*

Background

John Quincy Adams was born on July 11, 1767, becoming the second child and eldest son of the second President of the United States. Because of his father's diplomatic obligations, he was educated variously in Paris, Amsterdam, and Leiden, before returning to study at Harvard, graduating in 1787.

He studied law, and was admitted to the Boston Bar on July 15, 1790, and opened his own law practice. He never gained many clients, however, because his heart lay in politics. President Washington appointed him first as minister to Holland, and then to Portugal. Before he left for Portugal, he went on assignment to London, where his fiancée was waiting for him. His father was elected President, and cancelled his appointment, making him minister to Prussia instead. John Quincy married his fiancée, Louisa Catherine Johnson, on July 26, 1797, and the couple traveled to Berlin for Adams to take up his post.

On their return to America, Adams became a member of the Massachusetts State Senate and, in 1803, a member of the US Senate. In December, 1807, he was the only Federalist Senator to support the Embargo Act (which restricted trade with the British). His beliefs were against those of the Federalist party, and forced his resignation from the Senate on June 8, 1808; he intended to stay out of public life forever.

His sense of duty soon overcame his desire for privacy. In 1809, President Madison appointed him as minister to Russia, and in 1814, he was one of the US commissioners who negotiated the Treaty of Ghent, which ended the War of 1812. Next, he was appointed as minister to Great Britain, a role which he enjoyed until 1817, when President Monroe appointed him Secretary of State.

Adams' most significant achievement as Secretary of State was to help formulate the Monroe Doctrine, which stated that the American continents were "henceforth not to be considered as subjects for future colonization by any European powers."

Presidential record

Adams was inaugurated as the sixth President of the United States on March 4, 1825, after an extremely close battle with Andrew Jackson. The contest caused a split in the Democratic-Republican Party, and

Adams' group became the National Republicans. Jackson's group fought them bitterly throughout Adams' Presidency.

Inaugural promises

In his inaugural address, Adams proclaimed a spectacular national program, proposing the construction of highways, canals, weather stations, and a national university. He also advocated the financing of scientific expeditions and the erection of an observatory.

Congress, however, disagreed, declaring that such measures exceeded constitutional limitations, and Adams' hopes for a partnership of government and science were not to be realized during his lifetime.

1828 Election

Andrew Jackson avenged his defeat of 1824, by beating Adams by a landslide in 1828. Adams again sought to retire from public life, but was soon back, serving in the House of Representatives from 1831 until his death seventeen years later. During this time, he fiercely debated for the abolition of slavery, and consistently attacked Jackson. When Jackson received an honorary degree from Harvard, Adams wrote, "I would not be present to see my darling Harvard disgrace herself by conferring a Doctor's degree upon a barbarian and savage who could scarcely spell his own name."

On February 21, 1848, Adams suffered a stroke, collapsing on the floor of the House of Representatives, and was carried to the Speaker's Room, where he died two days later. Of his four children, only one, Charles Francis Adams, outlived him. Charles continued the family tradition, becoming a member of the House of Representatives and US Minister to England.

Andrew Jackson
1767–1845
7th President of the US (1829–37)
Democrat

Notable dates

Mar 15, 1767	*Birth*
Aug, 1791	*Married Rachel Donelson*
Jan 17, 1794	*Second marriage ceremony to Rachel Donelson*
Mar 4, 1829	*Presidential oath of office*
Mar 4, 1833	*2nd presidential oath of office*
Mar 4, 1837	*Retired from Presidency*
June 8, 1845	*Death*

Background

As a youngster, Andrew Jackson received little education, and joined the Revolutionary army aged just 13. During the war, he lost almost all of his immediate family and was himself taken prisoner by the British in April 1781. He was released when he fell ill with smallpox, on April 25.

After the war, he studied law and became public prosecutor in Nashville in 1788, rising to a judge of the Tennessee Supreme Court (1798–1804).

In 1791, he married Mrs Rachel Donelson Robards, who had been married to Lewis Robards. She believed that Robards had divorced her in 1790, but he did not actually do so until September 1793. Consequently, Jackson remarried her in 1794, and in later years, political opponents dubbed him an adulterer and his wife a bigamist. They never had children of their own, but in 1810, they adopted Rachel's month-old nephew, whom they named Andrew Jackson Jr.

Jackson was a man who fiercely believed in honor, and in a duel on May 30, 1806, killed a man who made derogatory comments about his wife. He himself was wounded in the duel, taking a bullet which remained in him for the rest of his life.

When war was declared against Britain in 1812, as major-general of the state militia, he won a decisive victory at Horseshoe Bend in 1814 against the Creek Indians, allies of the British. His volunteer army described him as "tough as hickory," gaining him the nickname "Old Hickory." As major-general of the regular army, he successfully defended New Orleans, making himself a national hero. In the Battle of New Orleans, 2000 British were killed or wounded, with little over 20 American casualties.

Presidential record

Jackson first stood for election as President in 1824. He took the highest popular vote, but did not have the majority of electoral votes, and the House of Representatives decided in favor of John Quincy Adams. Jackson won by a landslide in 1828, and sought to act as the representative of the common man. On the eve of his inauguration, he was thrown into mourning by the death of his wife. During his presidency, he would use his reputation as a hot-head at times, often going into rages. At other times, he appeared the consummate gentleman.

A strong leader

Jackson strengthened the power of the presidency. He used his veto more than any previous President, and rearranged his Cabinet to meet his own ends. His greatest battle was against the Second Bank of the United States, which he saw as a malignant monopoly. This proved to be a popular policy, and ensured his re-election in 1833.

He was a powerful diplomat, and successfully sought reparations from countries which had damaged US shipping during the War of 1812.

Native American policy

Throughout his presidency, Jackson pushed for Indian resettlement to free up frontier lands. He did much to push the Indians to the West of the Mississippi. In 1832, the Supreme Court invalidated Georgia's attempt to annex the territory of the Cherokee – Jackson refused to enforce the ruling.

People's President

While unpopular with many politicians, Jackson enjoyed enormous popularity from the public, because of his image as a plain-speaking champion of the common man. He did, however, survive an assassination attempt in January 1835, when he was shot at by Richard Lawrence.

He retired from office on March 4, 1837, and died in 1845 aged 78, of consumption and dropsy.

James Knox Polk

1795–1849
11th President of the US (1845–49)
Democrat

Notable dates

Nov 2, 1795	*Birth*
Jan 1, 1824	*Married Sarah Childress*
Mar 4, 1845	*Presidential oath of office*
Mar 4, 1849	*Retired from Presidency*
Jan 15, 1849	*Death*

Background

James Knox Polk was born on a farm near Pineville, North Carolina, on November 2, 1795, the oldest of 10 children. In 1815, he entered the sophomore class of the University of North Carolina, and graduated top of his class in 1818.

Polk returned home after his graduation, and began work in the law office of Felix Grundy. Grundy introduced him to Andrew Jackson, who was to prove an important influence in his life. Polk was admitted to the Bar in 1820, and began to practice in Columbia.

He was soon attracted to politics rather than law, and in 1823, he was elected to the Tennessee House of Representatives. He became a supporter of Andrew Jackson, and the two of them became so close that Polk acquired the nickname "Young Hickory" (Andrew Jackson's nickname being "Old Hickory").

Polk married Sarah Childress in a large country wedding on New Year's Day in 1824. Their marriage was successful, though they had no children.

In 1825, Polk was elected to the US House of Representatives, where he served seven consecutive terms. He offered fierce opposition to President John

Quincy Adams, who had defeated Andrew Jackson in the election of 1824. Polk became Speaker of the House in 1835, during Jackson's presidency, and remains the only Speaker to have become President.

Polk became the surprise Democrat nomination for President in 1844, on the sole strength that he supported the annexation of Texas, which the other candidates did not. During the election campaign, many people had never heard of him. "Who is James K. Polk?" even became a Whig campaign slogan. The key issue of the election remained Texas, which saw Polk through to a 40,000 votes victory over Senator Henry Clay.

Presidential record

Polk set out four measures that he wished to achieve while President. First, he wished to reduce the tariff, second to re-establish an independent treasury, third to wrest control of the entire Oregon Territory from the British, and finally, to acquire California from Mexico.

Polk the promise-keeper

In 1846, Polk reduced the tariff, with the introduction of the Walker Tariff. This was also the first US tariff to be based on the value rather than the quantity of imports. Less than a week after passing the tariff bill, Congress set up an independent treasury to oversee and distribute Federal funds. Within a year of his presidency, Polk had come through on half of his election promises.

Polk's next mission was to secure the Oregon Territory for the United States. He did not wish to go to war with the British over the matter, but made an offer to them instead. Britain rejected the offer, and war seemed possible, until the British made the unlikely move of making the same proposal to Polk that he had offered them. Polk accepted, and the Oregon Treaty of 1846 was signed. His third promise had become a reality.

This just left the small matter of California. Polk offered to buy it from Mexico, but was refused. On May 11, 1846, Polk declared war. The Mexican War ended in victory for the United States, and under the 1848 peace treaty, Mexico signed over not just California, but also parts of what are now Arizona, Colorado, Nevada, New Mexico, Utah, and Wyoming.

When Polk retired, he was satisfied that he had achieved all he had set out to. Exhausted by his presidency, Polk died a few months after leaving office.

Grover Cleveland

1837–1908
22nd and 24th President of the US (1885–89 and 1893–97)
Democrat

Notable dates

Mar 18, 1837	*Birth*
1861–65	*American Civil War*
Mar 4, 1885	*Presidential oath of office*
June 2, 1886	*Marriage to Frances Folsom*
Mar 4, 1889	*Retired from presidency*
Mar 4, 1893	*2nd presidential oath of office*
Mar 4, 1897	*Retired from presidency*
June 24, 1908	*Death*

Background

Stephen Grover Cleveland was born on March 18, 1837, in Caldwell, New Jersey, and dropped his first name while still a child. He was the fifth child in a family of four brothers and five sisters, and his father was a Presbyterian minister. Because of his father's job, he moved house regularly throughout his childhood, attending different schools up to the age of 14. When Grover was 16, his father died.

Grover did not attend college or university, but studied law while working for his uncle. In 1859, he was admitted to the New York Bar in Buffalo. When the American Civil War broke out in 1861, Cleveland continued to work as a lawyer, as money was needed to support his mother and her other children. He paid a substitute to take his place in the army, a practice which was legal, but which would be used against him later by his political enemies.

Cleveland worked his way up in legal circles, and was elected Mayor of Buffalo in 1881. He gained a reputation as an honest politician, resulting in the nomination as Governor of New York, a post he took in 1882.

Presidential record

Cleveland's reputation for honesty continued to grow, and he was nominated by the Democrats as their presidential candidate in 1884. His opponent, Republican James G. Blaine, had been implicated in a financial scandal, and many Republicans declared that they would vote for a Democratic candidate if he were an honest man. The election campaign centered not on the issues of the day, but on scandalous stories about the candidates. Cleveland won the election by 25,685 votes.

Reform

In his first term as President, Cleveland sought to reduce corruption, using the presidential veto to its full effect. He made sure that government appointments and pensions were granted on the basis of merit. He opposed many pension measures, particularly those for army veterans, as they had become riddled with fraud. Many healthy veterans claimed to be unfit for work, and Cleveland vetoed hundreds of claims.

The tariff issue

Industrialists wanted a high tariff to protect high prices, while farmers sought low tariffs so that they would avoid high prices for imported goods. Cleveland felt that tariffs should be reduced, and in his annual message, he asked Congress to lower them. Congress refused, but the nation became aware of Cleveland's intention to lower the tariffs, a move that was not popular.

On June 2, 1886, Cleveland cheered the nation with his marriage to Frances Folsom. His marriage to the 21-year-old is, to date, the only presidential marriage to have taken place in the White House.

Public opinion over the tariff issue was, however, sufficient for Cleveland to lose the presidential election of 1888.

Second term

Cleveland was re-elected in the election of 1892, making him the only President elected to two non-consecutive terms. His second term was plagued by a severe financial panic in 1893, which threw 4 million people out of work. America's gold reserves fell to dangerous levels, and Cleveland's popularity fell with them.

He did not stand for a third term, and spoke of his "poor old battered name" when he left the White House in 1897.

In his retirement, opinion of him gradually changed for the better. After a prolonged illness, he died on June 24, 1908. His last words are reported to have been, "I have tried so hard to do right."

Theodore Roosevelt

1858–1919
26th President of the US (1901–09)
Republican

Notable dates

Oct 27, 1858	*Birth*
Oct 27, 1880	*Married Alice Hathaway Lee*
Dec 2, 1886	*Married Edith Kermit Carow*
Mar 4, 1901	*Inaugurated as Vice-President*
Sep 14, 1901	*Presidential oath of office*
Nov 8, 1904	*2nd presidential oath of office*
Dec 10, 1906	*Awarded Nobel Peace Prize*

| Mar 4, 1909 | *Retired from presidency* |
| Jan 6, 1919 | *Death* |

Background

Theodore Roosevelt was born on October 27, 1858, in New York City. In his early years, he struggled against ill health, and his parents took him to Europe for a year from 1869–70 in the hope that the change of air would help to cure his asthma. The European trip developed a love of travel that was to remain with him until his death in 1919.

In 1876, he entered Harvard, graduating in June 1880. Later that year, on October 27, Roosevelt married his first wife, Alice Hathaway Lee.

Roosevelt threw himself into politics, serving three years as a member of the New York State Assembly. In 1884, he abandoned his political work for over two years to recover from personal tragedies. On February 14, his mother died from typhoid fever, and on the same day, his wife passed away just two days after the birth of their daughter, Alice. Roosevelt spent much of this time on his ranch in Dakota before returning, in 1886, to New York and to politics.

On a visit to London, he married his second wife, Edith Kermit Carow, on December 2, 1886. The couple remained together for the rest of his life, and raised five children.

Roosevelt's rise in politics was rapid. In 1889, he was appointed as a member of the Civil Service Commission, where he served until 1895. He was then elected President of New York City Police Board and, in 1897, became Assistant Secretary of the Navy. In May 1898, he resigned his political post to fight in the Spanish-American War. He was the lieutenant colonel of the "Rough Rider" Regiment, which he led on a charge at the Battle of San Juan, becoming one of the most recognizable heroes of the war. In November 1898, he was elected Governor of New York, where he served until 1900.

Aside from his political career, he will be remembered for his vast literary output — the author of 26 books, over 1,000 magazine articles and thousands of speeches and letters, but above all he is remembered as the namesake of the "Teddy Bear" because of his uncanny resemblance and his conservationism.

Presidential record

The Republican Party nominated Roosevelt for Vice-President in June, 1900, and he was elected to the post on March 4, 1901, serving under President McKinley. Less than a year after being elected Vice-President, he succeeded to the presidency after the assassination of President McKinley on November 14, 1901, becoming the youngest President in US history, aged 42. He brought new levels of power to the presidency, leading the United States toward progressive reforms, and initiating a strong foreign policy. He was re-elected to serve a full term in 1904.

Domestic policy

Roosevelt believed that it was the government's duty to arbitrate between the conflicting economic interests of the nation. He soon emerged as a "trust buster" by forcing the dissolution of a great railroad combination, and introducing a "Square Deal" policy for enforcing anti-trust laws.

Some of his most effective achievements as

President were in conservation. He set up Forest Reserves, particularly in the West, endorsed great irrigation projects, and ensured that a good deal of land was reserved for public use.

The world scene

Roosevelt ensured the United States its place in international politics.

His administration acquired the Panama Canal Zone in 1903 and initiated the construction of the Panama Canal.

He was responsible for preventing the establishment of foreign bases in the Caribbean, and reserved the sole right of intervention in Latin America to the US.

In 1905, Roosevelt acted as mediator between the Russians and the Japanese, resulting in a peace treaty in September of that year. For these services, he was awarded the 1906 Nobel Peace Prize.

Almost a third term

After his presidency, Roosevelt went on an African safari, after which he returned once more to politics, running, in 1912, for President once more, this time as the candidate for the Progressive Party.

During his campaign, Roosevelt was shot in the chest by a fanatic. He recovered and went on to fight for election. Despite his popularity with the nation, he lost to Democrat Woodrow Wilson, but polled more votes than Republican candidate, William Howard Taft.

Woodrow Wilson

1856–1924
28th President of the US (1913–21)
Democrat

Notable dates

Dec 28, 1856   *Birth*
June 24, 1885   *Married Ellen Louise Axson*
Mar 4, 1913   *Presidential oath of office*
1914–18   *World War I*
Dec 18, 1915   *Married Edith Galt*
Mar 5, 1917   *2nd presidential oath of office*

1919	Awarded Nobel Peace Prize
Mar 4, 1921	Retired from presidency
Feb 3, 1924	Death

Background

Woodrow Wilson was born in Staunton, Virginia, on December 28, 1856. Christened Thomas Woodrow, he soon dropped his first name. He was brought up in an intellectual family, and was regarded as a brilliant academic. He graduated from the College of New Jersey (now Princeton University) in 1879, and began to study law. He was admitted to the Bar of Georgia at Atlanta in 1882, and practiced law for a year before becoming a postgraduate student at John Hopkins University, Baltimore. In 1886, he received a Ph.D., and he remains the only US President to have achieved such a degree.

On June 24, 1885, Wilson married Ellen Louise Axson, with whom he had three daughters. Their marriage was generally regarded as a happy one, although it was shadowed briefly by Wilson's extramarital affair with Mary Allen Peck.

Wilson's academic career flourished, and he became Professor of several colleges and universities, culminating in his appointment as Professor of Jurisprudence and Political Economy at the College of New Jersey (Princeton), in 1896. In June, 1902, he was elected President of Princeton. The publicity he drew in this role attracted the attention of the Democratic Party, who offered him the nomination of Governor of New Jersey in 1910, a post he took on January 17, 1911.

He was nominated for President on July 2, 1912, and in the election, he received 435 of the 531 electoral votes, and was duly inaugurated on March 4, 1913.

Presidential record

Wilson had long been an academic, and had many ideas of how governments should be run. He broke with previous presidential practice by appearing in Congress in person, an approach that was to achieve significant results.

Wilson the legislator

Wilson steered three major pieces of legislation through Congress in his first term. His first victory was to see through the Underwood-Simmons Tariff, which reduced import duties for the first time in 40 years, and was accompanied by a graduated Federal income tax. After months of debate, the Federal Reserve Act was passed, providing the nation with an elastic money supply which it desperately needed. His anti-trust legislation established the Federal Trade Commission, which still regulates against unfair business practices.

He followed this with another wave of legislation in 1916, preventing child labor, and limiting railroad workers' hours to eight per day. These reforms, coupled with his policy of remaining out of the World War I, won him a second term.

World War I

The outbreak of war in Europe coincided closely with the death of Wilson's first wife. He married his second wife, Edith Galt, on December 18, 1915.

When a German submarine sank the *Lusitania* in May, 1915, Wilson sent letters of protest to Germany, but aggression against US shipping continued. On April 6, 1917, Wilson signed a declaration of war against Germany. America's involvement tipped the scales, and Germany surrendered on November 11, 1918.

Peace

After the war, Wilson went to Paris to try to build a lasting peace. At the Peace Conference, he argued strongly for the new League of Nations, and brought home the Treaty of Versailles, asking the Senate, "Dare we reject it and break the heart of the world?" The Senate did dare, and to date, the US has not joined the League of Nations.

Wilson became ill with a stroke on October 2, 1919, and never again fully functioned as President. His disabilities even prevented him from personally collecting the 1919 Nobel Peace Prize.

He retired from the presidency on March 4, 1921, and lived for nearly three years in Washington. He died from another stroke on February 3, 1924.

Harry S. Truman

1884–1972
33rd President of the US (1945–53)
Democrat

Notable dates

May 8, 1884	*Birth*
1914–18	*World War I*
June 28, 1919	*Married Elizabeth Virginia Wallace*
1939–45	*World War II*
Nov 7, 1944	*Elected Vice-President*

Apr 12, 1945	Presidential oath of office
Jan 20, 1949	2nd presidential oath of office
Jan 20, 1953	Retired from presidency
Dec 26, 1972	Death

Background

Harry Truman was born at Lamar, Missouri, on May 8, 1884. His parents gave him the middle initial "S", but no middle name, so that both of his grandfathers (Solomon Young and Anderson Shippe Truman) could claim that he was named after them.

His family was far from rich, and after leaving high school, he worked in various jobs. He was a member of the Missouri National Guard from 1905–11. Truman was sent to France in 1918 to fight in the World War I, and he was honorably discharged, ranked Major, in May, 1919.

Six weeks after he returned home, on June 28, 1919, he married his childhood sweetheart,

Elizabeth Virginia Wallace, and together they had one daughter.

Truman went into partnership with a friend in a men's haberdashery shop, but the business failed during the severe recession of 1921. Discouraged by this, Truman decided to seek a career in politics.

He served as county judge for Jackson County from 1922–24 and presiding judge from 1926–34, where he won a reputation for honesty. He took a seat in the Senate on January 3, 1935, where he remained until his nomination for Vice-President in 1944. He took the oath on January 20, 1945, and on April 12 the same year, became President following the death of Franklin D. Roosevelt.

Presidential record

The day after Truman took the oath to become President, he spoke to White House newsmen. He said, "Boys, if you ever pray, pray for me now. I don't know whether you fellows ever had a load of hay fall on you, but when they told me yesterday what had happened, I felt like the moon, the stars, and all the planets had fallen on me."

The end of the war

Truman had inherited the presidency at the very end of the World War II. Less than one month after he took the oath, Germany surrendered, on May 7, 1945. In July, he traveled to Potsdam, Germany, to meet Winston Churchill of Britain and Josef Stalin of Russia. The three leaders agreed to treat Germany as a whole for economic purposes and to prosecute German leaders for war crimes. While at Potsdam, Truman learned of the first atomic bomb test.

On his way home, Truman ordered American pilots to drop an atomic bomb on Japan, who refused to end the war. The first bomb fell on Hiroshima on August 6, and three days later, another was dropped on Nagasaki. Japan formally surrendered on September 2.

A new war starts

Soon after the World War II ended, the Cold War developed. The Communists took over many countries in Eastern Europe. Truman established the "Truman Doctrine" which guaranteed American aid to free nations resisting Communism.

Truman won a surprising victory in 1948, and started his second term on January 20. In 1949,

NATO was formed. The 12 countries who signed the Treaty agreed that an attack on one member would be considered an attack on them all. Other countries later signed, and Dwight Eisenhower served as its first Supreme Commander.

The Korean War

On June 25, 1950, Communist forces from North Korea invaded South Korea. On June 27, Truman announced that he had sent US planes and ships to help South Korea, in line with the Truman Doctrine. Ground forces followed on June 30, and by October, most of Korea was under UN control, but later that month, Chinese forces joined the North Koreans.

Truman ignored the advice from his generals to attack Chinese targets, preferring to limit the war to Korea and, in his mind, to prevent the outbreak of another World War. A prolonged and unpopular war followed, which officially ended on July 27, 1953, though a permanent peace treaty has never been signed.

Domestic issues

Truman's administration set up the CIA. As President, he pressed for an extensive reform program which he called the "Fair Deal," but most of his proposals were defeated by the predominantly Republican Congress.

He did not stand for President in the election of 1952, and left for a long, happy retirement. He died on December 26, 1972, in Kansas City, Missouri.

Dwight David Eisenhower

1890–1969
34th President of the US (1953–61)
Republican

Notable dates

Oct 14, 1890	*Birth*
July 1, 1916	*Married Mamie Geneva Doud*
1914–18	*World War I*
1939–45	*World War II*
1943–45	*Supreme Commander of Allied Expeditionary Force*
1945–48	*Army Chief of Staff*
1951–52	*Supreme Commander of European Defense*

Jan 20, 1953	Presidential oath of office
Jan 20, 1957	2nd presidential oath of office
Jan 16, 1961	Retired from presidency
Mar 28, 1969	Death

Background

David Dwight Eisenhower was born at Denison, Texas, on October 14, 1890, the third of seven sons. Christened David Dwight, he later transposed his forenames to become Dwight David.

He received a normal high school education before going to West Point Military Academy, from where he graduated in 1915. On July 1, 1916, he married Mamie Geneva Doud, and on September 24, 1917, she gave birth to their first son, Doud Dwight. Sadly, Doud Dwight died of scarlet fever, aged three.

During World War I, Eisenhower directed tank training programs, though saw no overseas action himself. After the war, he was stationed under Brigadier-General Fox Conner in the Panama Canal

Zone. Conner supported his admission to the Army's "leadership factory," the Command and General Staff School at Fort Leavenworth. In 1926, Eisenhower graduated first in his class of 275 army officers.

In 1933, he became an aide to General Douglas MacArthur, but he really came to prominence during World War II. When the Japanese attacked Pearl Harbor on December 7, 1941, Eisenhower held the rank of Brigadier-General, and was promoted to Major-General in March 1942. In November, 1942, he became Allied Commander-in-Chief for the invasion of North Africa, and on December 24, 1943, he was designated Supreme Commander of the Allied Expeditionary Force, responsible for the organization of the Allied forces' invasion of German-occupied Europe.

His diplomacy and planning skills brought about the D-Day landings and subsequent Allied victory against Hitler when Germany surrendered on May 7, 1945. A hero's welcome awaited him on his return to the United States in June.

With the establishment of NATO in 1950, Eisenhower was appointed Supreme Commander of the combined land forces, a role he took up in April, 1952.

Presidential record

Eisenhower resigned his NATO post in July, 1952, after being nominated as the Republican candidate for President. Despite the even balance of parties in the government, he won by a large majority, because of his popularity with the electorate. During his presidency, the government was preoccupied with foreign policy and the drive against Communism.

McCarthyism

America became obsessed with the "evils" of Communism. Senator Joseph McCarthy gained national attention in 1950 by charging that there were Communist spies in the State Department and the Army. McCarthy also attempted to ban books considered to be written by Communists, leading Eisenhower to urge, in a speech of 1953, "Don't join the book burners."

The Senate eventually took control, and condemned McCarthy in December 1954 for conduct unbecoming a Senator, but the public's fear of Communism would take much longer to subside.

Foreign policy

Eisenhower urged the world to harness nuclear power for peaceful means. In 1953, he set up a program called "Atoms for Peace" with the UN from which the International Atomic Energy Agency developed.

When Eisenhower was re-elected in 1957, with an even bigger share of the vote, he continued to adopt a diplomacy-led approach to foreign affairs. Near the end of his presidency, however, Fidel Castro seized all property owned by US companies in Cuba. Eisenhower was forced to break off diplomatic relations.

The space age

Eisenhower had long advocated a cost-cutting policy, limiting spending, but this had to change when the Soviet Union launched *Sputnik 1* on October 4, 1957. Americans were shocked that the Soviets had streaked ahead in the technology race. Eisenhower threw money into America's space program, with the result that on January 31, 1958, *Explorer 1* went into orbit.

Retirement

Eisenhower was the first President whose term of

office was limited by the Constitution. The 22nd Amendment, which became law in 1951, limits a President to two full terms, and Eisenhower left office in January 1961. After a series of heart attacks, he died of heart failure in March 28, 1969. He has gone down in history as one of America's great heroes.

Ronald Reagan

b.1911–
40th President of the US (1981–89)
Republican

Notable dates

Feb 6, 1911	*Birth*
1939–45	*World War II*
Jan 24, 1940	*Married Jayne Wyman*
June 28, 1948	*Divorce from Jayne Wyman*
Mar 4, 1952	*Marriage to Nancy Davis*

Jan 20, 1981   *Presidential oath of office*
Jan 20, 1985   *2nd presidential oath of office*
Jan 20, 1989   *Retired from presidency*

Background

Ronald Wilson Reagan was born on February 6, 1911, in Tampico, Illinois. From an early age, he developed an interest in performing, so it was little surprise that following his graduation from high school in 1928, he became an announcer for a radio station in Iowa.

As a sports presenter, Reagan traveled to southern California in 1937. While there, he made a screen test for Warner Brothers, who signed him to an acting contract.

Reagan made his film debut in *Love is on the Air* (1937), and soon became a star. Between 1937 and 1964, he starred in over fifty feature films. He met his first wife, Jane Wyman, while they were both appearing in Warner films, and they were married on January 25, 1940.

During World War II, Reagan joined the US Armed Forces, but was disqualified because of poor eyesight. He spent the majority of the war in Hollywood, making training films.

Reagan was elected president of the Screen Actors Guild, serving five consecutive terms from 1947–52. During this period, he divorced his first wife (1948) and, in 1951, met his second, Nancy Davis. The couple were married on March 4, 1952.

He gave up acting in 1966 to enter politics, and was elected Governor of the State of California the following year. He twice campaigned for the Republican presidential nomination unsuccessfully before finally winning in July 1980.

Presidential record

Reagan was inaugurated President on January 20, 1981, having defeated the incumbent President Carter. He inherited a very poor economy, with inflation running at 15% and unemployment at 7.5%. In his campaign, he had promised to balance the federal budget and cut income tax by up to 30%.

He claimed that cutting taxes would stimulate the stagnant economy so much that tax revenues would actually rise.

Recession and recovery

Congress approved most of Reagan's economic policies, but a recession struck in mid-1981, ending his hopes of a fast recovery. The Federal budget deficit grew, sparking the largest tax increases in history, and unemployment grew to the highest rate since 1941. Amid this crisis, an attempted assassination of the President happened. Reagan was shot in the chest in 1981, but he made a full recovery.

The economy began to recover in 1983, but the public grew tired of the tax burden.

Foreign affairs

Reagan declared that the Soviet Union held military superiority over the United States, and initiated a defense program to redress the balance. He supplied nuclear missiles to allies in Europe, causing tensions in US–Soviet relations.

In 1983, he ordered the invasion of Grenada after Grenadian Marxists overthrew the island's government. Victory in this conflict, coupled with the rapid economic upturn secured Reagan a second term.

Second administration

In his second term, Reagan's foreign policy was a strange mix of diplomacy and aggression. He advocated a space-based missile defense system (the "Star Wars" program), yet held four summit meetings with Soviet Premier Mikhail Gorbachev. In 1987, this led to the signing of a treaty to eliminate all US and Soviet intermediate nuclear forces.

The Iran-Contra affair

Reagan's administration came under fire over the sale of US weapons to Iran, and the use of the profits to help Nicaraguan rebels. As a result of the scandal, the White House Chief of Staff and the National Security Advisor were forced to resign, but Reagan said he knew nothing about the diverted funds.

Reagan escaped the scandal relatively unscathed. He left office with immense popularity, despite leaving his successor, George Bush, the problem of record trade and budget deficits.

Chapter Three

Untimely Death

Eight presidents have died or been killed whilst still in office: four at the hands of assassins and four as the result of illness.

It is said that every person over a certain age remembers where he or she was when John F. Kennedy was killed, for the event shocked the whole world.

The first President to be assassinated was Abraham Lincoln, shot by actor John Wilkes Booth in Washington on April 14, 1865.

James Garfield and William McKinley were also shot. Charles Guiteau shot James Garfield because he had not been given a diplomatic post he wanted and McKinley was killed because his assassin believed him to be the "enemy of the people."

No President is ever completely free of the risk of assassination and attempts were made to end the lives of Ronald Reagan, Franklin D. Roosevelt, Harry Truman, Andrew Jackson, and Gerald Ford.

Of the four who died from illness, one may have been a murder and two were more or less self-inflicted.

Officially, Warren Harding died following a stroke. However, the exact cause was never ascertained because his wife refused to allow an autopsy. Rumors soon spread that she had poisoned him to avoid his impeachment.

The two "self-inflicted" illnesses were those of Zachary Taylor, who went out in blistering heat and then over-indulged, and William Harrison, who got soaked in the rain and caught a chill.

The fourth to succumb to illness was Franklin D. Roosevelt, who collapsed at his desk and died soon after.

William Henry Harrison

1773–1841
9th President of the US (1841)
Whig

Notable dates

Feb 9, 1773	*Birth*
Nov 22, 1795	*Married Anna Tuthill Symmes*
1800–12	*Governor of Indiana Territory*
1811	*Defeated Indian uprising at Tippecanoe*
1816–19	*Member House of Representatives*
1819–21	*Ohio State Senator*
1828–29	*Minister to Colombia*
Nov 1840	*Elected President*
Apr 4, 1841	*Death*

Background

William Henry Harrison's father, Benjamin Harrison, was one of the signatories of the Declaration of Independence; his grandson, also christened Benjamin, became President (1889–93). William himself died after only a month in office.

He was born in Berkeley, Charles City County, Virginia, on February 9, 1773, the youngest son of Benjamin Harrison and Elizabeth Bassett.

He studied history and classics at Hampden-Sydney College but in 1791, he began to study medicine. Later that same year, following the death of his father, he suddenly decided to change course and joined the military. He obtained a commission as ensign in the First Infantry Regiment. In the following year, he was promoted to Lieutenant and served as aide-de-camp to General "Mad Anthony" Wayne. In December, 1793, he was part of an expedition to build Fort Recovery and he took part in a successful campaign against the Indians that ended with the Battle of Fallen Timbers on August 20, 1794, in which Wayne's men defeated Little Turtle and his force of 800 Indians.

Harrison became a Captain in May 1795 and six

months later married Anna Tuthill Symmes, the daughter of a former Chief Justice of the New Jersey Supreme Court. They were to have 10 children, four girls and six boys. Harrison resigned his commission in 1798 to take up his appointment, by President John Adams, as Secretary of the Northwest Territory and went to Congress as a territorial delegate the following year.

Indian fighter

When the Indiana Territory was formed in 1800 he was appointed Governor on May 12, a post he held for 12 years. He tried hard to avoid further wars with the Indians but, as his remit was to obtain title to Indian lands for settlers, it was inevitable that the Indians would retaliate. Tecumseh, Chief of the Shawnees, organized an uprising which ended with the Indians being defeated at the Battle of Tippecanoe on November 7, 1811.

In the War of 1812 against Britain, Harrison was made a Brigadier-General in command of all Federal forces in the Northwest Territory. He was promoted Major-General in March 1813 and achieved a decisive victory against the combined British and Indian forces at the Battle of the Thames on October

5, 1813. Tecumseh, who had been commissioned Brigadier-General by the British, was killed during this battle and the Indians never again put up any serious resistance.

On May 19, 1828, President John Quincy Adams appointed Harrison first United States Minister to Colombia. He arrived in Colombia in February 1829 and was there little more than a month when he was recalled by Andrew Jackson.

He then retired to live in Ohio where he took an interest in Whig politics. He was elected to Congress (1816–19), the Ohio Senate (1819–21) and the US Senate (1825–28). As a national hero who held noncommittal political views, Harrison appealed to the Whigs and they nominated him as one of their three presidential candidates in 1836. The Whigs lost to the Democrat Martin Van Buren, but in 1840, they nominated Harrison their sole candidate, largely presenting him as a simple Indian fighter of humble background. The ploy seemed to work for Harrison won with 234 electoral votes to his opponent's 60.

Presidential record

At the aged of 68, Harrison was the oldest man to be

inaugurated for a first term, a record he held until 1981 when President Reagan was inaugurated. Harrison still holds the record for the longest inaugural speech and the dubious distinction of serving the shortest presidency.

Daniel Webster edited Harrison's inaugural address, which was filled with classical allusions. Webster managed to make some cuts and thereafter boasted that he had killed "17 Roman proconsuls as dead as smelts, every one of them."

Harrison's inauguration ceremonies at the Capitol on March 4, 1841, took place in a cold drizzle. Harrison rode on horseback through driving rain to the Capitol and then delivered his address, without the protection of a hat or an overcoat. He caught a cold which developed into pneumonia and he died a month later on April 4, 1841, the first President to die in office.

Zachary Taylor
1784–1850
12th President of the US (1849–50)
Whig

Notable dates

Nov 24, 1784	*Birth*
June 21, 1810	*Married Margaret Mackall Smith*
1812–14	*Frontier campaigns against Indians and British*
1832	*Black Hawk War*
Sep 23, 1846	*Capture of Monterrey*
Feb, 1847	*Battle at Buena Vista*
Nov 7, 1848	*Elected President*
July 9, 1850	*Death*

Background

Nicknamed "Old Rough and Ready," Zachary Taylor was a renowned Indian fighter and hero of the Mexican War (1846–48), who gained his presidential ticket on his fighting record rather than for any political prowess.

He was born in Montebello, Orange County, on November 24, 1784, the third son of Richard Taylor and Sarah Dabney Strother. Little is known of his early life on the Kentucky frontier before he joined the Army in 1806. Within two years he was commissioned First-Lieutenant. By 1838, he was commanding officer of all Florida forces. In 1840, he was given command of the Army in the south west and by 1846, he was a Major-General.

On June 21, 1810, he married Margaret Mackall Smith, the daughter of a rich planter. She followed him from posting to posting until they eventually settled down in Baton Rouge, Louisiana, in the early 1840s. They had six children.

During the Mexican War, his troops crossed the Rio Grande and captured the Mexican city of Matamoros. Just four months later, on September 23, 1846, they captured Monterrey. The Mexican

General Pedro de Amoudia surrendered to Taylor on condition that he and his forces could have time to retreat and not be pursued for eight weeks. Taylor's agreement of these terms was not well received by President Polk in Washington who ordered Taylor to remain in northern Mexico, play a defensive role, and turn over most of his men to General Winfield Scott, who was ordered to capture Mexico City. In February, 1847, Taylor disobeyed orders to march towards Buena Vista where he won a major victory despite being outnumbered by four to one.

The Whigs saw in Taylor, who was now a national hero, a potential presidential candidate and he became their nomination at the 1848 convention. He defeated Lewis Cass and Martin Van Buren in the general election and was inaugurated as President on March 5, 1849.

Presidential record

Taylor's short administration was rife with problems, the most worrying of which was the status of the newly acquired Mexican territories. He was in favor of the admission of California and New Mexico to the Union as anti-slave states but leaders in the South were against this and threatened to remove their support. The Compromise of 1850, designed to solve the slavery problem, was not to his liking (he owned a hundred slaves himself), but he died before the measure could be passed by Congress.

As a general rule he was out of touch with Congress and took the view that he should accept any legislation it passed. Even on matters on which he had firm, opposing views, he did not take a stand.

There were also problems caused by improper conduct by some members of his Cabinet. This was humiliating to Taylor who prided himself on his honesty and he planned to reorganize the Cabinet, but he died before this could be accomplished.

He spent the intensely hot day of July 4, 1850, eating large amounts of cherries and other fruits, washed down with ice-cold water after attending the Fourth of July ceremonies at the Washington Monument. For the next five days he had severe stomach pains and he died on the morning of July 9.

James Garfield

1831-81
20th President of the US (1881)
Republican

Notable dates

Nov 19, 1831	*Birth*
Nov 11, 1858	*Married Lucretia Rudolph*
1863–80	*Member of House of Representatives*
Mar 4, 1881	*Presidential oath of office*
Sep 19, 1881	*Death*

Background

James Abram Garfield, the youngest son of Abraham (Abram) Garfield and Eliza Ballou was born at Orange, Ohio on November 19, 1831. His father died when he was just two years old, leaving the family in poverty. His mother continued to run the family farm and the children had to work as farm hands and go to school when they could during the winter. In 1848 and 1849, Garfield drove canal boat teams, and then, for the next two years, he attended Geauga Seminary in Chester, working as a carpenter during school vacations.

He then went to Hiram Eclectic Institute (now Hiram College), and paid his way by teaching. In September 1854, he entered Williams College, Massachusetts, from which he graduated in 1856. He then returned to the Western Reserve Eclectic Institute to teach Latin and Greek. He must have been good at his job for within a year he was made Principal of the school.

On November 11, 1858, he married Lucretia "Crete" Rudolph, the daughter of a local farmer and carpenter.

He became a supporter of the Republican Party

and was elected to the Ohio State Senate in 1859. From 1858, he studied law when he could and was admitted to the Ohio Bar in 1860.

Civil War hero

Garfield fought in the Civil War, being commissioned as Lieutenant-Colonel of the 42nd Regiment of Ohio Volunteers. In November 1861, he was promoted to Colonel and given command of the 18th Brigade of the Army of Ohio a month later. At a time when Union military victories were few, he led a brigade to a successful conclusion against Confederate forces at Middle Creek, Kentucky. He became a Brigadier-General and fought at Shiloh and Chickamauga and was now a Major-General of volunteers.

President Lincoln persuaded him to resign his commission and enter Congress, for it was easier to find Major-Generals than successful Republicans for Congress. He won re-election for 18 years to become the leading Republican in the House.

Presidential record

In the Republican search for a presidential candidate in 1880, some 28 unsuccessful ballots were held.

Finally, it was decided that a compromise candidate was needed. On the 36th ballot, James Abram Garfield was declared the party's candidate.

He won the election and was inaugurated President on March 4, 1881. His proud 79-year-old mother attended the ceremony, the first mother of a President to do so.

Civil service reform

He supported the call for civil service reform, a stance that was not well received by many of his own party. He strengthened Federal authority over the New York Customs House, eventually ousting Senator Roscoe Conkling, and in so doing helped the movement to reform government patronage.

He attacked political corruption and, in spite of his short term in office, succeeded in winning the presidency some renewed prestige.

Assassination

After only four months in office, Garfield was fatally shot in the back on July 2, 1881, at the Baltimore and Potomac railroad station, by a disgruntled office-seeker, Charles Jules Guiteau, because Garfield had given preferential treatment to radical Republicans.

Garfield was taken to the White House where doctors using unsterilized instruments probed for the bullet, which had lodged in a muscle. When this failed they tried a metal detector that had been invented by Alexander Graham Bell. The search was unsuccessful and it was not until later that it was realized this was because Garfield was lying on a bed with metal springs! He died on September 19, 1881, and his assailant was hanged for his crime.

William McKinley

1843–1901
25th President of the US (1897–1901)
Republican

Notable dates

Jan 29, 1843	*Birth*
Jan 25, 1871	*Married Ida Saxton*
1877–90	*Member of House of Representatives*
1890	*McKinley Bill*
1892–96	*Governor of Ohio*
Nov 3, 1896	*Elected President*
1897	*Dingley Tariff Act*
1898	*Spanish-American War*

Nov 6, 1900   *Elected for second term*
Sep 14, 1901   *Death*

Background

The man destined to be the 25th President was born in Niles, Ohio, on January 29, 1843, the third son of William McKinley and Nancy Campbell Allison. His early schooling was in Niles, and when the family moved to Poland, Ohio, in 1852, he entered the Union Seminary there. Seven years later he went to Allegheny College, Meadville, Pennsylvania. He had to leave college after only a year because of ill health, so he returned to Poland to teach.

He then became a Post-Office clerk up to the start of the Civil War, when he enlisted as a private in the Union Army. He served as aide-de-camp to Colonel Rutherford B. Hayes (later to become 19th President), who encouraged McKinley's political aspirations. After the war he attended law school at Albany, New York, was admitted to the Ohio Bar in 1867, and began to practice in Canton, Ohio.

On January 25, 1871, he married Ida Saxton, the daughter of a local banker. Ida, a frail girl, became a chronic invalid, suffering with phlebitis and epilepsy after the deaths of their two daughters in early childhood and the loss of her mother. She was a never-ending source of anxiety to McKinley for the rest of his life.

McKinley was elected to the House of Representatives in 1876, taking his seat on March 4, 1877, where his attractive character, intelligence, and honesty served him well. As a Congressman, he called for a high tariff policy to protect America from foreign competition and this was implemented in the McKinley Bill of 1890 which raised US tariffs to the highest level.

With the support of wealthy industrialist Mark Hanna, he was elected Governor of Ohio in 1891 and served two terms. Hanna was also instrumental in McKinley winning the Republican presidential nomination in 1896. In later years, the newspapers caricatured McKinley as a small boy being led by his "nursie" Hanna.

During the presidential election, Hanna campaigned vigorously and raised huge sums of money to support the campaign. McKinley stayed at his home in Canton, daily addressing the hordes of people who came to see him. McKinley won the election with the highest majority of popular votes for 18 years.

Presidential record

Soon after taking office, McKinley called a special session of Congress to increase customs duties (the Dingley Tariff). Other domestic issues were overshadowed by foreign affairs.

Increasing influence overseas

Following newspaper reports of the Cuban insurrection and the suffering inflicted by Spain, a public outcry put pressure on McKinley to intervene; after the sinking of the American battleship *Maine* in Havana harbor, McKinley advocated neutral intervention. On April 25, 1898, Congress voted for three resolutions to liberate the people of Cuba from Spanish rule. After the short war that ensued, American territory was expanded by annexing Havana, the Philippines, Puerto Rico, and Guam.

American influence overseas was asserted further when McKinley sent American troops to help protect foreigners in China during the Boxer Rebellion and when he twice intervened to protect American property interests in Nicaragua.

Shot by an anarchist

He was elected for a second term in 1900, but the inauguration day, on March 4, 1901, was marred by Mrs McKinley suffering an epileptic fit during the ball. This was not an uncommon occurrence but McKinley always refused to have his wife hidden away and had her at his side at State dinners, calmly placing a lace handkerchief over her face when she had a fit.

Six months later, on September 6, 1901, McKinley was shot twice in the chest by an unemployed mill worker, Leon F. Czolgosz, whilst visiting the Pan-American Exposition at Buffalo. He died eight days later. Czolgosz said that he shot McKinley because he was an "enemy of the people, the good working people."

The first modern President

McKinley used to be regarded as a rather weak

President. Theodore Roosevelt said that McKinley had no more backbone than a chocolate éclair, but his decisiveness in the declaration of war against Spain and his authority over his Cabinet belie this. During his presidency, America built up a strong marine and merchant navy, became a colonial power, adopted the monetary gold standard, and became a significant player in world trade.

John F. Kennedy

1917–63
35th President of the US (1961–63)
Democrat

Notable dates

May 29, 1917	*Birth*
Aug 1943	*Awarded Purple Heart*
1947–52	*Member of House of Representatives*
Nov 4, 1952	*Elected US Senator for Massachusetts*
Sep 12, 1953	*Married Jacqueline Lee Bouvier*

1953–60	*Senator for Massachusetts*
May 6, 1957	*Awarded Pulitzer Prize*
Nov 8, 1960	*Elected President*
Mar 1, 1961	*Founded The Peace Corps*
Aug 5, 1963	*Nuclear Test Ban Treaty*
Nov 22, 1963	*Assassination in Dallas*

Background

John Fitzgerald Kennedy, the second son of the millionaire diplomat and industrialist, Joseph Kennedy, and Rose Elizabeth Fitzgerald, was born in Brookline, Massachusetts, on May 29, 1917.

He was educated at private schools and then at the prestigious Choate School in Wallingford, Connecticut. In 1936, he entered Harvard, from which he graduated in 1940. He expanded his thesis on Great Britain's unpreparedness for war into a best-selling book, *Why England Slept*. During World War II, he gained distinction in the Navy as a torpedo boat commander in the Pacific. When his boat was sunk by a Japanese destroyer near the Solomon Islands in 1943, Kennedy, who was seriously injured, led the survivors to safety through dangerous waters to an island from which they were later rescued.

He was elected Democratic representative in 1947 and senator for Massachusetts in 1952. In the following year, on September 12, 1953, he married Jacqueline Lee Bouvier, the daughter of a stockbroker of French ancestry. The couple had met at a dinner party a year before and he, as he himself put it, "leaned across the asparagus and asked her for a date."

Throughout his life, JFK was dogged with health problems, a fact that was carefully hidden from the American public. In 1955, whilst recuperating from a back operation, much of the time being strapped to a board, he wrote *Profiles In Courage*, which won the Pulitzer Prize in history in 1957. The book also brought him to public notice.

Presidential record

JFK became the first Roman Catholic, and the youngest person, to be elected President by narrowly beating Richard Nixon in 1960. His win was due in no small part to a series of television debates with Nixon, Kennedy looking handsome, tanned, and confident and Nixon, who refused make-up, appearing tired and tense.

White House restorations

Kennedy and his wife set about refurbishing the White House. With her excellent taste, Jackie Kennedy oversaw the restorations. Top performers were invited to entertain at the White House, a practice that has been adopted by subsequent "tenants." She almost slipped up on one thing, however. One of the first things the Kennedys removed was a picture of Mrs Eisenhower that hung in the entrance hall. It was hastily recovered and put back on the wall when the Eisenhowers came to dinner!

Stand off with the Soviets

Kennedy was largely criticized for the ill-fated Bay of Pigs, the Cuban invasion in 1961 in which he attempted to oust Fidel Castro and restore a right-wing government. Kennedy assumed "sole responsibility" for the fiasco, but in reality it occurred because the Joint Chiefs-of-Staff had unanimously advised the young President that it would spark a revolution against Castro. In the following year, American intelligence discovered Soviet missile sites in Cuba, and Kennedy decreed, at the risk of starting a nuclear war, that Soviet ships carrying weapons to the area would be intercepted. After a period of worrying international tension, Soviet shipment of weapons ceased shortly afterwards, the weapons were withdrawn from Cuba, and a partial nuclear test ban treaty was agreed in 1963.

His presidency embraced a feeling of optimism and public service backed by energy, and his economic policies launched America on its longest period of expansion since World War II.

Death in Dallas

Kennedy was assassinated in November 1963 while driving in a motorcade with his wife in Dallas. Two bullets hit him, one in the head and one at the base of the neck. He was dead on arrival at Parkland Memorial Hospital. The assassination was allegedly perpetrated by Lee Harvey Oswald, but controversy as to the veracity of this abounds to this day. Oswald was himself killed at point-blank range by Dallas night club owner, Jack Ruby, just two days later whilst being heavily escorted by police.

Chapter Four

Thrust Into The Spotlight

ACCORDING TO SHAKESPEARE "Some men are born great, some achieve greatness, and some have greatness thrust upon them" (*Twelfth Night*).

Certainly, several Vice-Presidents have had "greatness thrust upon them" when their boss's terms were suddenly and unexpectedly terminated.

The first to step into a dead man's shoes was John Tyler on the death of William Harrison. As such a move was unprecedented, Tyler's opponents stated that, according to the Constitution, Tyler should have stepped down. They proposed that he be retained as acting President, but Tyler successfully claimed all the rights and privileges of office, thus setting an important precedent for the transfer of the presidency.

Since then many others have had to adopt the mantle of power unexpectedly.

The assassinations of Abraham Lincoln, James Garfield, William McKinley, and John F. Kennedy brought Andrew Johnson, Chester Arthur, Theodore Roosevelt, and Lyndon Johnson to the fore.

When Theodore Roosevelt was sworn in following the assassination of William McKinley, he was the youngest man to become President up to that time.

John Tyler, Millard Fillmore, Calvin Coolidge, and

Harry Truman were thrust into the spotlight upon the deaths in office of William Harrison, Zachary Taylor, Warren Harding, and Franklin D. Roosevelt.

The only occasion when the sudden elevation from Vice-President to President was not due to the death of the incumbent was when Richard Nixon resigned and Gerald Ford had to take the helm.

John Tyler
1790–1862
10th President of the US (1841–45)
Whig

Notable dates

Mar 29, 1790	*Birth*
1811–16	*Member of the state legislature*
Mar 29, 1813	*Married Letitia Christian*
1825–27	*Governor of Virginia*
1835–42	*Second Seminole War*
Apr 4, 1841	*Became President on the death of William Harrison*

June 26, 1844	Married Julia Gardiner
1845	Annexation of Texas
Jan 18, 1862	Death

Background

John Tyler was born in Charles City County, Virginia on March 29, 1790, the second son and the sixth of eight children of John Tyler and Mary Marot Armistead.

His family were politically active and, after briefly attending William and Mary College in 1806, the young man studied law with his father until 1808, when his father became Governor of Virginia. He was admitted to the Bar in 1809 in spite of the fact that, at 19, he was too young to do so. Two years later, he began his political career when he was elected a member of the Virginia House of Delegates.

On March 29, 1813, he married Letitia Christian, the daughter of a planter. They had eight children. Letitia died in 1842 and Taylor remarried two years later, on June 26, 1844. His new wife, with whom he had seven children, was Julia Gardiner. She was 30 years younger than Tyler, which certainly gave the press something to write about!

Tyler was a Congressman (1817–21), State Governor (1825–27) and a US Senator (1827–36). In July 1826, as Governor of Virginia, he delivered an oration at the funeral of Thomas Jefferson. In 1840, the Whigs nominated Tyler for Vice-President, a move they hoped would bring support from southern states'-righters who were against the policies advocated by Andrew Jackson.

Presidential record

In 1840, Tyler was elected Vice-President to William Harrison and became President a year later when Harrison died. He was the first Vice-President to become President by the death of his predecessor and he was soon nicknamed "His Accidency" by his detractors. His opponents wanted him to be acting President only, but Tyler successfully claimed all the rights and privileges of office.

His first act on becoming President was to grant a

pension of 25,000 US dollars to Mrs Harrison, the first time that such a pension had been granted to a President's widow.

Calls for impeachment

The Whigs were optimistic that Tyler would adopt their program but they were quickly disappointed. Immediately on taking office Tyler found himself in opposition to his own party and all but one of his Cabinet resigned when he vetoed bank proposals advocated by the Whigs. The Whigs retaliated by expelling Tyler from their party and nicknaming him "Old Veto." There were demands for his resignation and calls for impeachment, but Tyler hung on to office. He was now a President without a party, but in spite of this, his administration achieved a great deal.

A year later, when he vetoed a tariff bill, Tyler became the first President to face impeachment. John Quincy Adams and a committee he headed reported that Tyler had misused his power of veto, but the resolution failed.

In May 1844, he was nominated for President by the Tyler Democrats of Baltimore, but he withdrew his candidature three months later. After attending the inauguration of President James Polk on March 4, 1845, John Tyler retired to Sherwood Forest, his 1,200-acre plantation, but remained active in local affairs right up to his death from bilious fever on January 18, 1862, at the age of 71.

Many people were of the opinion that Tyler did not have the political skills required of a President and that his sudden elevation to the presidency showed, for the first time, the importance of having a Vice-President qualified to take on "the top job" should it prove necessary. Today Tyler is best remembered for the bills that admitted Texas and Florida to the Union.

Millard Fillmore

1800–74
13th President of the US (1850–53)
Whig

Notable dates

Jan 7, 1800	*Birth*
Feb 5, 1826	*Married Abigail Powers*
1833–42	*Member of House of Representatives*
1848–49	*Comptroller of New York State*
Nov 7, 1848	*Vice-President*
July 9, 1850	*Succeeded as President*
Mar 4, 1853	*Retired from presidency*

| Feb 10, 1858 | Married Caroline Carmichael McIntosh |
| Mar 8, 1874 | Death |

Background

Millard Fillmore is often described as a nonentity but he must have had great fortitude, for he educated himself and became a lawyer. He became a member of the State Assembly in 1829, was elected to Congress in 1833, and became a comptroller of New York State in 1847. He was Vice-President to Zachary Taylor, 1849–50, and became President on Taylor's death. Not a bad achievement for a nonentity!

He was born in Locke (now Summerhill), Cayuga County, New York, on January 7, 1800, the eldest son of Nathaniel Fillmore and his first wife, Phoebe Millard. His early education was basic and he worked on his father's farm until being apprenticed to a cloth dresser when he was 14. He taught himself to read, occasionally stealing books to do so. The apprenticeship was nothing short of slavery but eventually Fillmore managed to borrow $30, to pay his obligation to his employer and, released from his apprenticeship, he walked 100 miles home to be with his family for Christmas.

When he was 18, he managed to obtain a clerical position with a local judge and soon after began to study law himself. In 1823, he was admitted to the Bar and he entered politics five years later, encouraged by his wife Abigail.

Abigail Powers was a schoolteacher and Fillmore, two years her junior, had been one of her pupils. They were engaged for eight years, during which Fillmore struggled to become a lawyer, and were married on February 6, 1826. When her husband became President, Mrs Fillmore, who had a sizeable library of her own, was horrified to discover that there were no books in the White House. She successfully appealed for a grant from Congress with which she established the White House Library.

In 1830, Fillmore moved his law practice to Buffalo where he was asked to run for the New York State Assembly. He served three terms and was elected to the House of Representatives in 1832. He served four terms in Congress, lobbied, unsuccessfully, for vice-presidential nomination in 1844 and, in the same year, was unsuccessful in an election for Governor of New York. In 1847, he became New York State Comptroller, an election that he won by such a wide margin it was almost inevitable that he would be elected Vice-President in the following year.

Presidential record

Millard Fillmore and President Zachary Taylor did not meet one another until after the election – when they did, there was an immediate clash of personalities. They held differing views on all major issues and Fillmore eventually found himself excluded from the decision-making processes.

A little over a year later, Fillmore became President in July 1850, on the sudden death of Zachary Taylor. Fillmore's appointment heralded a sudden shift in policy and Taylor's Cabinet resigned.

The Compromise of 1850

As a Congressman, Fillmore supported the abolition of the domestic slave trade but as President he signed the Fugitive Slave Act (known as the Compromise of 1850), which was designed to appease both sides – this made him unpopular in the North. Many of the northern Whigs could not forgive Fillmore for having signed the Compromise and this deprived him of the presidential nomination in 1852 and led to the death of the Whig party.

In 1853, he sent a US Navy fleet, under the command of Commodore Matthew Perry, to force Japan to change its isolationist stance and to enter into trade and diplomatic relations. His foreign policy also included efforts to keep the Hawaiian Islands free from European control and he refused to support an invasion of Cuba by southerners who wanted to establish a slave-based economy there.

In 1856, he was the presidential candidate for the American Party, nicknamed "The Know-Nothing Party," whose main policy was to oppose immigration. Overwhelmingly defeated in the election, he retired to Buffalo and never again ran for public office.

On February 10, 1858, he married a widow, Mrs Caroline Carmichael McIntosh (Abigail having died in 1853). After a long honeymoon in Europe, mainly in Paris and Madrid, they returned to Buffalo where he lived quietly. He made occasional public appearances up to his death, at the age of 74, on March 8, 1874, almost completely forgotten by the American people.

Chester A. Arthur

1830–86
21st President of the US (1881–85)
Republican

Notable dates

Oct 5, 1829	*Birth*
Oct 25, 1859	*Married Ellen Lewis Herndon*
Sep 19, 1881	*Presidential oath of office*
1882	*Chinese Exclusion Act*
Jan 16, 1883	*Pendleton Civil Service Act*
Mar 4, 1885	*Retired from presidency*
Nov 18, 1886	*Death*

Background

The eldest son of Reverend William Arthur, a Baptist preacher who had emigrated from Ireland, and Malvina Stone, Chester Alan Arthur was born in Fairfield, Vermont, on October 5, 1829. There is, however, the possibility that he was actually born in Canada where his parents lived for a time. If so, he would be the only President not to have been born in America and therefore not eligible for this office.

He entered Union College, Schenectady, New York, in September 1845, graduated in July 1848, and went to teach at North Pownal, Vermont, where he was appointed Principal a year later. Like many others destined to be President, he was admitted to the Bar, and practiced law in New York City.

On October 25, 1859, he married Ellen Lewis Herndon, the daughter of Commodore William Lewis Herndon, who achieved fame by exploring the Amazon. Mrs Arthur died in January 1880 at the young age of 42; they had three children but the first died when only two years old.

Support for the spoils system

During the Civil War, Arthur, now active in local politics, was appointed Quartermaster-General for the State of New York and, in 1871, President Grant made him Customs Collector of the port of New York. The Custom House was renowned for its notorious abuse of the spoils, or patronage, system; Arthur, although honorable in both his personal life and his career, supported the system in which employees were selected not on merit but because of their political affiliation and he employed more staff than was needed purely because they were loyal to the New York Republican leader Senator Roscoe Conkling.

At the Republican National Convention of 1880, Arthur and Conkling worked with the "Stalwart" faction to renominate Ulysses Grant for a third term as President. They failed but reluctantly accepted the nomination of Arthur for the vice-presidency, an act that did not prove popular with the public.

Presidential record

Arthur was thrust into the presidency on the assassination of James Garfield in 1881. During his brief tenure as Vice-President, Arthur openly sided with Conkling in a bitter battle against Garfield over New York patronage. But after taking the oath as President, he was so upset by public apprehension at his appointment that he determined to show he was above machine politics and became a reformer, much to the surprise of his critics.

He became a firm supporter of civil service reform, prosecuted corruption in the postal service, and avoided his old political friends. In 1883, Congress passed the Pendleton Civil Service Act, which provided for the open selection of government employees based on merit, regardless of religion, race, or politics. He vetoed the Chinese Exclusion Bill of 1882, which barred Chinese from acceptance as immigrants, because it went against a treaty between America and China. Congress overrode Arthur's veto and the bill became law. His presidency was good, if unremarkable, but he was responsible for several reforms in the Civil Service, initiated the rebuilding of the US Navy, and was the instigator of several reciprocal trade agreements with other countries.

Many had viewed Arthur's accession to office with trepidation, but by 1884, when the next presidential election was held, his administration had won respect.

Unfortunately, he did not have any strong following amongst the leaders of the Republican Party. Although suffering from an incurable kidney disease, he allowed his name to be put up for nomination but was defeated by James G. Blaine. He retired from office on March 4, 1885.

Elegant Arthur

Arthur is generally remembered as the best-dressed President, being nicknamed "Elegant Arthur." Not only was he well dressed – he had some 80 suits in his wardrobe – he wanted the White House to look good as well. He hired New York's leading designer, Louis Comfort Tiffany, to transform the shabby building, which he described as "a badly kept barracks," into a place befitting the highest office in the land. One of his first acts as President was to employ a French gourmet chef to work in the White House. Chester Arthur also has an unusual claim to fame in that he was the first to install an elevator in the White House!

Calvin Coolidge

1872–1933
30th President of the US (1923–29)
Republican

Notable dates

July 4, 1872	*Birth*
Oct 4, 1905	*Married Grace Anna Goodhue*
1907–08	*Mayor of Northampton, Masschusetts*
1912–15	*Member of Massachusetts Senate*
1914–15	*President of Massachusetts Senate*
1916–18	*Lieutenant-Governor of Massachusetts*

1916–18	Governor of Massachuasetts
1919–20	Vice-President
Jan 5, 1933	Death

Background

John Calvin Coolidge first came to public notice when, as Governor of Massachusetts, he ended the 1919 Boston police strike by calling in the militia. Coolidge, a man of few words but not afraid of acting boldly, defended his action stating there was "no right to strike against the public safety by anybody, anywhere, anytime" – the strike was crushed. The action brought him public acclaim and the vice-presidential nomination for the Republicans in 1920.

Coolidge was born in Plymouth, Vermont, the first child and only son of village storekeeper Colonel John Calvin Coolidge and his first wife, Victoria Josephine Moor. He graduated from Amherst College with a B.A.

degree in June, 1895, in spite of the fact that he had originally failed the entrance exam; he began practicing law in 1897. Entering politics as a council man, he made his way slowly and methodically up the political ladder to become Mayor of Northampton, State Senator, Lieutenant-Governor, and Governor of Massachusetts (1919–20).

On October 4, 1905, Coolidge married Grace Anna Goodhue, a teacher of deaf children. They had two sons, John in 1906 and Calvin in 1908. Grace was bright and cheerful, almost the exact opposite of her taciturn husband.

At the Republican National Convention of 1920, delegates nominated Coolidge for Vice-President in retaliation against the party bosses who had selected Warren Harding to run for President.

Presidential record

At 2:30 on the morning of August 3, 1923, while visiting his family, Coolidge was told of the unexpected death of Warren Harding. By the light of a kerosene lamp, his father, who was a Justice of the Peace, administered the oath of office. Coolidge then went back to bed!

Soon after taking office, Coolidge forced the resignation of all suspected profiteers who had benefited during the corruption that was rife during Harding's short term in office. He helped lower taxes with his support for the Revenue Acts of 1924 and 1926, and he reduced the national debt.

In 1924, Coolidge was re-elected to serve a further term for which the inauguration took place on March 4, 1925. The oath was administered by former President William Howard Taft – it was the first inauguration to be broadcast.

During his second term, he supported the noble but impractical 1928 Kellog-Briand Pact which renounced war as a means of settling international disputes. He refused to be renominated in 1928 and retired to Northampton to write his autobiography.

Man of few words

Coolidge was a man of few words and a passive President because he believed man's actions were of little import in the grand scheme and claimed that "the best government is the least government."

He often sat silent through interviews and once explained his reticence to speak with "I say only 'yes' or 'no' to people. Even that is too much. It winds them up for twenty minutes more." In spite of his lack of oratorical ability, he was one of the first to make good use of the new medium of radio to get his policies across to the public and he was amazingly popular throughout his presidency.

It is said that, on one occasion a White House dinner guest bet his wife that she could get him to say at least three words. Without even looking at her, Coolidge said quietly, "You lose."

Coolidge died of a coronary thrombosis on January 5, 1933. When the writer Dorothy Parker was told he was dead she said, "How can they tell?"

Lyndon B. Johnson

1908–73
36th President of the US (1963–69)
Democrat

Notable dates

Aug 27, 1908	*Birth*
Apr 10, 1937	*Elected to House of Representatives*
Nov 17, 1934	*Married Claudia Alta Taylor (Lady Bird)*
June 1942	*Awarded Silver Medal for gallantry*
May 1948	*Elected to US Senate*

Nov 9, 1960	Elected Vice-President to John F. Kennedy
Nov 22, 1963	Presidential oath of office
1964	Civil Rights Act
Jan 20, 1965	Second inauguration
1964	Voting Rights Act
1965	Medicare Bill
Jan 20, 1969	Retired from the presidency
1971	Memoirs (The Vantage Point) published
Jan 22, 1973	Death

Background

Lyndon Baines Johnson, the elder son of Samuel Ealy Johnson Jr and Rebekah Baines, was born in Stonewall, Texas. Although poor, his family were politically active, so LBJ, as he was often called, became interested in politics at an early age. After leaving high school in 1924, he hitchhiked around the country doing odd jobs for a living. He then studied at Southwest Texas State Teachers College in

San Marcos and subsequently taught speaking and debating at a school in Houston.

Entry into politics

In 1932 he became secretary to Congressman Richard M. Kleberg, having assisted in his congressional campaign. On November 17, 1934, he married Claudia Alta Taylor, known since childhood as "Lady Bird." In the following year President Roosevelt appointed him director of the National Youth Administration in Texas and in 1937 he was elected a Democratic representative. For the next ten years, he represented the 10th Congressional District of Texas.

During World War II, he served briefly in the Navy as a lieutenant commander and was awarded a Silver Star for gallantry in action in New Guinea in June 1942. In the following month, he returned to Washington when President Roosevelt ordered all Congressmen on active service to return to their offices.

LBJ was elected to the Senate in 1948 and became minority leader of the Senate in 1953, the youngest in the Senate's history. In the following year, when the Democrats won control, he became majority leader.

In 1960, by now something of a legend in politics, he campaigned to become the Democratic nomination for President but lost to John F. Kennedy. Kennedy invited him to be his running mate and, when Kennedy became President in 1961, LBJ was elected Vice-President. As Vice-President, he represented Kennedy on visits to Europe, Asia, and Africa, and accompanied the President on his fateful trip to Dallas.

Presidential record

LBJ became President following the assassination of John F. Kennedy on November 22, 1963. On the same day, Johnson took the presidential oath on board the presidential jet Air Force One, that was carrying Kennedy's body back to Washington. The oath was administered by US District Judge Sarah T. Hughes, the first time that a woman had officiated.

One year later, he was elected for a second term with a large majority, the widest popular margin in American political history.

Social and welfare policies

No stranger to poverty himself in his early days, he

sympathized with the poverty of others and led the fight against deprivation, delinquency, development of depressed areas, and the removal of obstacles to the right to vote. With the Civil Rights Act (1964) and the Voting Rights Act (1965), his administration greatly improved the rights of African Americans. With the 1965 Medicare amendment to the Social Security Act, he provided medical care for millions of elderly Americans. His aim was "to build a great society, a place where the meaning of man's life matches the marvels of man's labor." In his first years in office, he initiated changes in education, housing, crime prevention, and urban renewal in one of the most comprehensive legislative programs ever seen.

LBJ was a great supporter of America's exploration of space and in December 1968, three astronauts successfully orbited the moon.

The Vietnam War

LBJ devoted the whole of his life to politics and successfully promoted many social changes in his pursuit of his dream of "A Great Society" for the American people. In spite of his efforts, there was much racial unrest and, in spite of campaign pledges, America's increased involvement in the Vietnam War overshadowed his legislative record of social reform. There were active protests and LBJ faced growing unpopularity. On March 31, 1968, he announced an end to the bombing of North Vietnam and that he had decided not to seek re-election.

When he retired from office, he planned to devote his time to the quest for peace and the end of Communist aggression. Unfortunately, he did not live to see his dream fulfilled, for he died suddenly of a heart attack at his Texas ranch on January 22, 1973. An agreement to end the war in Vietnam was signed less than a week later.

Gerald Ford

b.1913–
38th President of the US (1974–77)
Republican

Notable dates

July 14, 1913	*Birth*
Oct 15, 1948	*Married Elizabeth (Betty) Ann Bloomer*
1973–74	*Vice-President*
Aug 7, 1974	*Took the presidential oath*
Jan 20, 1977	*Retired from presidency*

Background

Gerald Rudolph Ford was born in Omaha, Nebraska, on July 14, 1913. His original name was Leslie Lynch King, but his parents divorced when he was just two years old. His mother moved to Grand Rapids, Michigan, where she married Gerald R. Ford, president of the Ford Paint and Varnish Company, who adopted the boy and gave him his name. Ford never knew he had been adopted until he was 17, when his real father turned up at the restaurant where Ford was working as a part-time waiter and introduced him to his stepmother and half-sister.

After attending South High School in Grand Rapids, he studied at Michigan University and starred in their football team. After graduating in 1935, with a dual degree in economics and political science, he received offers to become a professional footballer, but declined and went to Yale where he served as an assistant coach while studying for his law degree, which he received in 1941.

Shortly after the onset of World War II he joined the US Naval Reserve, where he attained the rank of Lieutenant-Commander and accrued 10 battle stars. After the war, he returned to Grand Rapids where he practiced law. In 1948, he married Elizabeth "Betty" Ann Bloomer, a 30-year-old divorcee, who taught dancing and worked as the fashion co-ordinator for a department store in Grand Rapids.

He became a Republican member of the House of Representatives (1949–73) and gained a reputation for integrity. He was re-elected successively and became House minority leader in 1965. In 1963, President Johnson appointed him as a member of the Warren Commission to investigate the assassination of President Kennedy in November 1963. On the resignation of Spiro Agnew in 1973, following revelations about tax evasion, President Richard Nixon appointed Ford Vice-President, the first Vice-President to take office during an administration.

Presidential record

Following Richard Nixon's resignation after the Watergate scandal, Gerald Rudolph Ford was inaugurated President on August 9, 1974. It was the first time in American history that the President had not been elected either as President or as Vice-President. In the same year, Ford granted Nixon a full pardon "for all offenses against the United States," an act that made him very unpopular. Ford voluntarily appeared before a sub-committee of the House of Representatives to explain his unpopular decision, the first time that a serving President had formally testified before such a committee.

Improving foreign relations

Gerald Ford set out to restore confidence in the presidency and faced the almost impossible task of overcoming inflation, reviving the economy, coping with massive energy shortages, and dealing with economic recession. Despite opposition from a largely Democratic Congress, he vetoed a number of non-military appropriations because they would have increased the heavy budgetary deficit.

He worked hard for the improvement of relations between the United States and the People's Republic of China. He provided aid to Israel and Egypt and persuaded these countries to accept an interim truce agreement. Relations with the Soviet Union continued to ease, and he and Leonid Brezhnev agreed to new limitations on nuclear weapons.

The first public debates

In the fall of 1976, he agreed to public debates with

Jimmy Carter, the Democratic nominee, the first time that such debates had occurred. Although sincere and honest, Gerald Ford was no intellectual and possessed a clumsiness of movement which made him rather accident prone. This, according to President Johnson, was due to the fact that Ford had received kicks to the head in his footballing days. Although generally regarded as a nice guy, his political talents were not impressive and Jimmy Carter won the 1976 presidential election, albeit by a narrow margin. Gerald Ford retired to private life after a troubled and difficult term but having done much to restore the dignity and reputation of the presidency. On Inauguration Day, President Carter opened his speech with the words: "For myself and for our nation, I want to thank my predecessor for all he has done to heal our land."

Chapter Five

Mixed Fortunes

PRESIDENTS HAVE ENJOYED periods of political success often interspersed with mistakes, scandals, and other events that made them unpopular.

Take any presidency at random and you will find low points. Thomas Jefferson had his first Vice-President, Aaron Burr, tried for treason; his successor, James Madison, had problems with the British and became unpopular in New England; and Harry Truman had to make the hard decision to drop the atomic bomb on Japan.

You will also find highs. Under James Monroe and the "era of good feelings," the number of states increased; Theodore Roosevelt instituted the Panama Canal; and Nixon was in power when the Americans became the first to land on the moon.

Richard Nixon is possibly the most dramatic example of mixed fortunes. After losing the 1960 presidential election, he was regarded as a has-been. But his win in 1968 and again in 1972, earned him the name "The Comeback Kid." But events then turned sour with the Watergate affair that forced his resignation.

"Comeback Kid" has also been applied to Bill Clinton. Serious charges made against him would have ended the careers of most people but Clinton always had the ability to bounce back. In the end, however, what could have been regarded as a successful presidency has been down-graded forever by Clinton's mistakes in his personal life.

Whether times are good or bad, being President is a stressful occupation. John Quincy Adams said of the presidency that he could "scarcely conceive a more harassing, wearying, teasing condition of existence" – but that is the nature of the job.

Andrew Johnson

1808–75
17th President of the US (1865–69)
Democrat

Notable dates

Dec 28, 1808	*Birth*
May 17, 1827	*Married Eliza McCardle*
Nov 8, 1864	*Elected Vice-President*
Apr 15, 1865	*Took the presidential oath*
1867	*Tenure of Office Act*
Mar 4, 1869	*Retired from presidency*
July 31, 1875	*Death*

Background

Andrew Johnson was born on December 29, 1808, in Raleigh, North Carolina, the youngest child of Jacob Johnson and Mary (Polly) McDonough. He was just four years old when his father died.

Self-education

Although he had no formal schooling, Johnson was apprenticed to a tailor in 1822 and the other apprentices taught him the alphabet. He borrowed books and taught himself to read, a long and hard process. Two years later, he ran away, his employer putting up a $10 reward for his return. He worked as a journeyman tailor in Laurens, South Carolina, and opened a tailor's shop in Greenville, Tennessee in 1826.

On May 17, 1827, he married 16-year-old Eliza McCardle who taught him how to write and improved his reading skills. She also helped him to make sound investments in land and property and she continued to administer such affairs for the rest of their lives.

He began taking parts in debates at the local academy, eventually entering politics; by the age of 21 he was elected an alderman, thanks largely to his organization of a working man's party, and became Mayor of Greenville (1830–33). Later he was a member of the Legislature (1835), State Senate (1841), and Congress (1843) where he proved to be an advocate for small farmers. He was made Governor of Tennessee in 1853 and became a Senator in 1857.

In 1862, President Lincoln appointed him Military Governor of Tennessee, in recognition of his loyalty to the Union despite being denounced by his constituents who dubbed him a traitor. In 1864 the Republicans nominated him, even though he was a Democrat, for Vice-President.

Presidential record

Towards the end of the Civil War, Abraham Lincoln was assassinated and Andrew Johnson became the third Vice-President to succeed to the office of President through death.

At odds with Congress
Unfortunately Johnson's views were too old-fashioned for the time and he was no match for the radical Republicans in Congress. One of the first

things they did was to refuse entry to any senator or representative from the old Confederacy and then they passed measures to extend civil rights to former slaves. Johnson tried to veto the legislation because he believed black people to be inferior to whites, but he was beaten, the first time that Congress had overridden a President on an important issue.

His pleas for reconciliation after the Civil War were opposed by Congress, who wanted to keep the Southern states under military rule. In March 1867, Congress passed the first of the Reconstruction Acts which provided for military administration of the southern states. Johnson managed to delay this program.

In the following year, he tried to remove the Secretary of War, Edwin Stanton, from his post and in doing so went against the Tenure of Office Act brought in by the radicals, which denied the President the right to dismiss top officials without consulting the Senate. As a result, Johnson became the first US President to be impeached by the Senate, but the vote fell short of the required two-thirds majority and he was acquitted by just one vote.

The worst President?

Johnson retired from the presidency on March 4, 1869 and two years later made an unsuccessful bid for election to the Senate. He tried again in 1875 and this time he was successful, taking his seat on March 5, the only former President to do so. Later that year he returned to Greenville but soon after suffered a stroke and died on July 31, 1875.

Whilst Johnson's rise to power, having had no formal education, was impressive, his racial intolerance made him unsuited for the presidency after the Civil War. He was unable to accept the new order of things because they conflicted with his own view and, as a result, he is generally considered to be the worst President.

Ulysses S. Grant

1822–85
18th President of the US (1869–77)
Republican

Notable dates

Apr 27, 1822	Birth
1846–48	Fought in the Mexican War
Aug 22, 1848	Married Julia Dent
1863–65	Commanded Union army in the Civil War
Apr 1865	Received Lee's surrender at Appomattox
1867–68	Secretary of War
Mar 4, 1869	Inauguration
Nov 5, 1872	Elected for second term
July 23, 1885	Death

Background

Ulysses Simpson Grant was born Hiram Ulysses Grant in Point Pleasant, Ohio on April 27, 1822, the eldest son of tanner Jesse Root Grant and Hannah Simpson.

His father got him a place in the Military Academy at West Point and it was here that his name was changed to Ulysses S. Grant when the Congressman who sponsored him got the name wrong on the entry form. Although Grant was not happy at West Point, he graduated in 1843 and became a brevet Second-Lieutenant in the 4th US Cavalry near St Louis, Missouri. There he met Julia Dent, whose brother was his room-mate; they were married on August 22, 1848. They had four children.

He first saw action in the Mexican War (1846–48) under Zachary Taylor, then settled as an unsuccessful farmer in Missouri on land given to Julia by her father; he then entered the real estate business in partnership with his wife's cousin, Harry Boggs. He lasted there until 1860 when he got a job in his father's hardware and leather goods store until the outbreak of the Civil War in 1861. He rejoined the Army and was appointed to lead an undisciplined volunteer regiment, later named the 21st Illinois Volunteers, which he soon knocked into shape. On February 16, 1862, he won the first major

Union victory when Fort Donelson in Tennessee surrendered.

After one of the bloodiest battles of the war, at Shiloh, he went on to victories at Vicksburg and Chattanooga. In March 1864, he was appointed General-in-Chief and just 13 months later he received Lee's surrender at Appomattox Court House on April 9, 1865; he was made a full General in the following year, the first officer to attain the rank of full General since Washington.

On August 12, 1867, President Andrew Johnson made Grant the Secretary of War and on May 21 the following year he was unanimously nominated for President at the Republican National Convention in Chicago.

Presidential record

Revered as a great military hero, Grant's victory in the 1868 presidential election was almost a foregone conclusion. Grant entered the White House on March 4, 1869; although he was the youngest elected President up to that time, it was expected that his administration would mark an end to the confusion and agitation of previous years but this turned out not to be the case. Although a great military leader, he approached government like a military campaign, made some very bad appointments, and appeared lost in the world of politics, being once described as "a puzzled pathos, of a man with a problem before him of which he does not understand the terms."

In spite of his shortcomings, his administration, marred by scandal, and remembered for its corruption and bitter partisan politics, Grant achieved a second term with a large majority over Horace Greeley in 1872.

He retired from the presidency on March 4, 1877, and embarked on a world tour with his wife and youngest son, Jesse. Everywhere he went he received an outstanding reception.

On returning to America, he sought nomination for a third term as President (the first to do so) but was defeated. He then became a partner in a financial company, which went bankrupt, and he lost a lot of money. Having discovered that he had cancer of the throat, he began writing his memoirs to pay off his debts. He finished writing on July 19, 1885 and died, just four days later, on July 23, 1885.

On his death the New York Tribune said that "the greatest mistake of his life was the acceptance of the presidency."

Rutherford B. Hayes

1822–93
19th President of the US (1877–81)
Republican

Notable dates

Oct 4, 1822	*Birth*
Dec 30, 1852	*Married Lucy Ware Webb*
Mar 5, 1877	*Inauguration as President*
Mar 4, 1881	*Retired from presidency*
Jan 17, 1893	*Death*

Background

Rutherford Birchard Hayes was born, the youngest son of farmer and storekeeper Rutherford Hayes and Sophia Birchard, in Delaware, Ohio, on October 4, 1822. His father had died 77 days previously.

When he was six, Rutherford attended school in Delaware and then at Norwalk Academy, Ohio. From 1837, he was educated at Isaac Webb's School in Middletown, Connecticut and then at Kenyon College, Gambier, Ohio, where he gained a B.A. degree in 1842. A year later he entered Harvard Law School from which he graduated in 1845. For five years he practiced law in Lower Sandusky (now Freemont), Ohio and then, from 1849–61, was a successful lawyer in Cincinnati where he represented several fugitive slaves.

On December 30, 1852, he married Lucy Ware Webb, the daughter of a local doctor, and between 1853 and 1874 they had eight children. Of the eight children only one was a girl, which gave rise to Hayes describing himself and his wife as being "in the boy business."

Hayes served with distinction in the Union Army during the Civil War, in the 23rd Ohio Volunteer

Infantry Regiment; he was wounded in action at the battle of South Mountain, and attained the rank of brevet Major-General before resigning from the Army in 1865.

He entered Congress (1865–67) and became Governor of Ohio for three terms (1868–72 and 1876–77). In June 1876, the Republican National Convention in Cincinnati nominated Hayes for President.

Presidential record

Although many famous Republican speakers, including the author Mark Twain, supported Hayes in the 1876 presidential election, he expected the Democrat Samuel J. Tilden to win. Early returns seemed to prove him right in this assumption and he went to bed thinking he had lost. But following a dispute over voting returns, known as the Hayes-Tilden affair, Congress established an Electoral Commission to determine the outcome. Hayes won by just one vote, having 185 electoral votes to Tilden's 184.

Restoring dignity to the presidency

During his term, the United States regained much of the commercial prosperity lost in the crash of 1873. He withdrew Federal troops from areas of the South still occupied, and promised not to interfere with elections in the former Confederacy. His policies included reform of the civil service and the establishment of official integrity following eight years of corruption, but he was unable to get his legislation through Congress.

He did, however, manage to restore confidence and respectability to the presidency, which had declined badly during the terms of Johnson and Grant.

No wine at the White House

Henry Adams, grandson of President John Quincy Adams described Hayes as "a third-rate nonentity, whose only commendation is that he was obnoxious to no one."

The truth is that he was religious, honest, modest, and did not smoke or drink. He and his wife, a strong supporter of the temperance movement, banished all alcoholic drinks from the White House, an act that delighted the Women's Christian Temperance Union and gained her the nickname "Lemonade Lucy."

Another name she gained was that of the "First Lady," termed in a magazine article about the presidential inauguration, and the term has been used for the wife of the President ever since.

Hayes announced in advance that he would serve only one term as President and in 1881 he returned to his home in Freemont, Ohio to devote himself to humanitarian causes, particularly in the areas of prison reform, education for black people, and the welfare of Civil War veterans.

On January 14, 1893 he suffered a heart attack whilst returning home from a business trip; he died three days later.

Warren G. Harding

1865–1923
29th President of the US (1921–23)
Republican

Notable dates

Nov 2, 1865	*Birth*
1904–06	*Lieutenant-Governor of Ohio*
1915–20	*Senator from Ohio*
Nov 2, 1920	*Elected President*
July 8, 1891	*Married*
1921	*Immigrant Quota Act*
Aug 2, 1923	*Death*

Background

Warren Gamaliel Harding was born on November 2, 1865 in Corsica (later renamed Blooming Grove), Ohio, the eldest son of Dr George Tryon Harding and his first wife, Phoebe Elizabeth Dickerson.

He learned the printing trade in the *Caledonia Argus* which his father bought in 1875. In 1880, he began studying at Ohio Central College from which he graduated two years later. During his time at the college he edited the school yearbook and became a horn player in the school band. After a short spell in teaching, he worked for the *Marion Mirror*, the family having moved to Marion a short while previously.

In 1884, he and two partners acquired the *Marion Daily Star* and he bought out his partners two years later.

In 1899, he gained a seat in the Ohio State Senate and became Lieutenant-Governor in 1902. He then returned to journalism until 1914 when he was elected to the US Senate.

On July 8, 1891, he married divorcee Florence Mabel Kling De Wolfe, whom Harding nicknamed "Duchess." Up until then the *Marion Daily Star* had been barely successful but his wife took control when

Harding fell ill and the newspaper prospered. Harding then became a director of several important businesses and took part in Republican Party events.

By 1919, Harding was being promoted as a presidential candidate. He assured the 1920 Republican National convention that there was nothing in his past that could affect his nomination. What he did not tell them was that he had a 7-month-old daughter by Nan Britton, a 22-year-old from Claridon, and that he was also involved with a married woman in Marion. Later Britton was given a job in Washington, DC, and the affair continued, with frequent liaisons in the Oval Office, right up to Harding's death.

Presidential record

Harding won the Republican nomination and the presidency in 1920, campaigning against American membership of the League of Nations. Several distinguished Republicans, however, signed a manifesto, stating that a vote for Harding was a vote for the League.

Harding's administration was responsible for America's isolationism between the two World Wars, largely because he invariably signed the bills brought by Republicans in Congress. They got rid of wartime controls, cut taxes, instituted high protective tariffs, and put tough controls on immigration. They also convened the Washington Conference of 1922 to discuss reducing the strength of world navies.

Scandals and corruption

Unfortunately, Harding, who had been selected by a lobby of influential businessmen as a pliable candidate, did not possess the talents required of a President. He even admitted to friends that he did not have the abilities required of such high office. His Cabinet was largely unsupervised, inefficient, and dishonest, and many lesser appointments were made because they were friends and not for their political expertise.

There were a series of scandals involving corruption among members of his Cabinet, the main one being the Teapot Dome Scandal which involved the secret leasing of land for oil exploration, especially at Teapot Dome, Wyoming, by Secretary of the Interior Albert B. Fall. Several members of the administration, including the Attorney General, resigned, criminal proceedings were instituted, and Fall received a prison sentence.

Mysterious and opportune death

Worried by the claims of corruption being made against his government, Harding, on June 20, 1923, began a transcontinental tour to assuage his waning popularity. An able public speaker, he undertook a strenuous series of speaking engagements all over the country. Whilst travelling by train from Seattle to California, he suffered an attack of food poisoning on the night of July 27, 1923. Four days later, in the Palace Hotel, San Francisco, he had a sudden heart attack as his wife was reading the newspaper to him. His death was so unexpected that it was rumoured that Mrs Harding had orchestrated it to avoid him facing possible impeachment.

Richard Nixon

1913–1994
37th President of the US (1969–74)
Republican

Notable dates

Jan 9, 1913	*Birth*
June 1940	*Married Thelma Catherine Ryan*
1942–45	*Service in US Navy*
1947–50	*Member of the House of Representatives*
1951–52	*Senator for California*
Nov 5, 1952	*Became Vice-President*
Nov 5, 1968	*Elected President*

June 17, 1972	*Watergate burglary*
Nov 7, 1972	*Elected for second term*
Aug 8, 1974	*The first President to resign from office*
Apr 22, 1994	*Death*

Background

Richard Milhous Nixon was born in Yorba Linda, California, the second of five sons of Francis (Frank) Anthony Nixon and Hannah Milhous. In 1919, Frank Nixon's lemon grove failed and the family moved to Whittier, California where Frank started a grocery business and gas station.

After attending Whittier High School, from which he graduated with honours in 1930 and received a prize as the most outstanding pupil in his class, Richard Nixon studied at Whittier College, graduating in 1934, and then at Duke University Law School in Durham, North Carolina.

In November 1937, he was admitted to the

California Bar, became a lawyer in Whittier, was taken into partnership in 1939 and worked briefly in the Office of Price Administration in Washington.

On June 21, 1940, he married Thelma "Pat" Catherine Ryan whom he had met when they both joined a community theater group. Although she enjoyed an active social life, she was shy, disliked speaking in public, and was not completely happy being in the public eye.

Tricky Dicky

Nixon served in the US Navy with the Fleet Air Command in the South Pacific and attained the rank of Lieutenant-Commander. After the war he was elected to the US House of Representatives in 1947 and again in 1949. During this period he gained a reputation for being a none-too-scrupulous adversary, using smear techniques to gain advantage, which earned him the nickname "Tricky Dicky."

He became a Senator in 1950 and two years later General Dwight Eisenhower selected him to be his running mate and he became Vice-President (1953–61). On a visit to Moscow in 1959, he achieved some notoriety as a result of his heated exchanges with Nikita Khrushchev. He narrowly lost the presidential election to John F. Kennedy in 1960. In 1962, he stood for the governorship of California but was defeated so he retired from politics to practice law in New York City. He returned to politics in 1968, standing in the presidential election which he won by a narrow margin and was re-elected in 1972 with a large majority, one of the largest in American history.

Presidential record

Richard Nixon's period in the White House was marred by civil disorders and inflation. He tried to reduce inflation by cutting Federal spending but, in spite of his efforts, the annual budget deficits became the largest up to that time. There was also widespread agitation over America's continuing war in Vietnam, but he achieved the withdrawal of US troops from that theater in 1973. This, his provision of economic aid to encourage Far Eastern countries to become more self-sufficient, and improved relations with the USSR were positive achievements.

In May 1972, he visited Moscow, the first such visit by an American President, which resulted in the SALT I nuclear arms limitation agreement, plans for joint scientific and space ventures, and a trade accord. In 1974, disengagement agreements were formed between Israel and its opponents, Egypt and Syria.

Watergate leads to resignation

Nixon resigned, the first President to do so, when threatened with impeachment following the 1972 Watergate scandal, when it was revealed that agents for his presidential campaign had burgled the Democrat's party headquarters on June 17, 1972. Investigations by the *Washington Post*, a grand jury, and two special prosecutors showed people close to Nixon were involved and that he knew of attempts to cover up the scandal. At first he claimed executive privilege for senior White House personnel to prevent them from being questioned about the affair. Further credibility was lost when he refused to hand over tapes of conversations which showed he had tried to divert the investigation.

On August 8, 1974, he announced that he would resign to start "that process of healing which is so desperately needed in America." Just one month after his forced resignation he was given a full pardon by President Gerald Ford.

Bill Clinton

b.1946–
42nd President of the US (1993–2001)
Democrat

Notable dates

Aug 19, 1946	*Birth*
1975	*Married Hillary Rodham*
Nov 3, 1992	*Elected President*
1993	*North American Free Trade Agreement*
Nov 5, 1996	*Re-elected President*

Background

William "Bill" Jefferson Clinton was born William Jefferson Blythe IV on August 19, 1946, in Hope, Arkansas. His father, William Blythe, died in a road accident before he was born and he was adopted by his stepfather, Roger Clinton of Hot Springs, Arkansas, whom his mother married when Bill was just four years old.

He studied at Georgetown University, receiving a bachelor's degree in international affairs in 1968. He then studied at Oxford University for two years, before going to Yale Law School where he received a law degree in 1973. He achieved great things as a student and also proved to be an excellent saxophone player – a skill he demonstrated at several private and public functions throughout his career.

Whilst at Yale Law School, he met Hillary Rodham and they were married in 1975. An ardent feminist, Hillary refused to change her surname for five years after the wedding. A brilliant attorney in her own right, Hillary Clinton played a leading role in the presidency and maintained a high degree of resilience amid all of the accusations that have been fired at her husband over the years.

Bill Clinton entered politics, having been inspired to this calling by a meeting with President Kennedy whilst in high school, as State Attorney General in Arkansas (1977–79) and became Democratic governor (1979–81, 1983–92). When elected Governor of Arkansas, he was the youngest governor in America for 40 years.

In 1992, he won the Democratic presidential nomination against severe criticism of his alleged draft deferment during the Vietnam War and charges concerning extramarital affairs.

Presidential record

When he entered the White House, after beating George Bush and Reform Party candidate Ross Perot, Bill Clinton became the youngest man since John F. Kennedy to be elected President.

On November 5, 1996, Clinton was elected for a second term, defeating Republican nominee Bob Dole.

Successes at home and abroad
Bill Clinton's record as President includes substantial intervention in the trouble spots of the world,

especially the Middle East and Ireland. In 1994, he successfully achieved the reinstatement of Haitian President Jean-Bertrand Aristide and committed American forces to a peacekeeping initiative in Bosnia and Herzegovina.

At home, he turned the greatest deficit in American history into a period of economic prosperity. In 1993, legislation was passed to increase tax on the wealthy and to make cuts in government programs. Later that year, he obtained Congressional approval for the North American Free Trade Agreement, which created a free-trade zone between America, Canada, and Mexico.

Controversy and scandal

Throughout his political life, Clinton was dogged by charges of extramarital affairs. These included a civil suit against him by Paula Jones in 1991 alleging sexual harassment and a highly publicized report of a sexual relationship with Monica Lewinsky, a White House intern, which emerged in January 1998. The possibility of impeachment was raised when it was proved that Clinton had lied about the Lewinsky affair and that he had tried to suborn a witness.

His career was also marred by allegations of

financial wrongdoing in the Whitewater real estate project in Arkansas, in which three of Clinton's former business associates were found guilty of fraud and conspiracy.

Even up to the end of his second term, Clinton courted criticism when, as one of his final acts, he struck a legal deal to avoid prosecution for lying about the Lewinsky affair. He also granted pardons to over a hundred people, including Susan McDougall, his former Whitewater business partner, and his brother Roger, who had been convicted for the possession of cocaine.

Few Presidents can have survived such a prolonged period of accusations of impropriety, but the American people seem to have taken the view that Bill Clinton's public and private lives are separate issues.

Chapter Six

Once is Enough

THE PRESIDENT OF THE UNITED STATES is a powerful man, but there are limits to his power. Above all, he is limited by the voice of the people. He may have a nuclear arsenal, the world's best-equipped military, and preside over an economy second to none, but every four years it is the ordinary American who stands up and says if he stays or goes.

For a number of Presidents, the news on election day has been bad. The ultimate political office brings with it the ultimate responsibility – the Oval Office is where the buck really does stop. An economic collapse, such as the Great Depression, can finish a presidency even though its origins may lay in events that took place many years before that administration began. Similarly, a foreign crisis which a President could not possibly have prevented can be his downfall.

It may seem harsh to judge a man for events he could not control but it is an essential element of the presidency. The man, and perhaps one day the woman, who is elected President is ultimately the servant of the people. He is entrusted with the fate of the nation for a term of four years and becomes, in a sense, the embodiment of the American people in one individual. Stepping into the office of President a man gives up a degree of his personal freedom – he is judged by impossible standards and held to account for events outside of his control. It is essential that this should be so.

In this chapter, find out about the men who, justly or unjustly, incurred the displeasure of the American people and fell, or were pushed, from the highest executive office in the world.

Martin Van Buren

1782–1862
8th President of the US (1837–41)
Democrat

Notable dates

Dec 5, 1782	*Birth*
Feb 21, 1807	*Married Hannah Hoes*
Nov 6, 1832	*Elected Vice-President*
Nov 8, 1836	*Elected President*
Mar 4, 1841	*Retires from presidency*
Jul 24, 1862	*Death*

Background

Martin Van Buren was the son of a tavern keeper and was born in Kinderhook, New York. He attended Kinderhook Academy and, aged just 14, began to study law. He was admitted to the Bar at the remarkably young age of 21 and went on to develop a successful law practice in Kinderhook. He specialized in defending local small businesses and farmers against large land owners and soon became involved in local politics.

In 1807, Van Buren married Hannah Hoes, a distant cousin. Their happy marriage produced four sons before Hannah's death in 1819. By this time Van Buren had been elected to the New York Senate in Albany as a Republican-Democrat. Factional fighting in the party first benefitted Van Buren as he was appointed Attorney General in 1816 and then cost him that office in 1819 when a political rival became Governor.

Two years later, Van Buren was elected to the Senate and left Albany for Washington. After a successful first term he was re-elected in 1827 and became involved with the growing political career of future President Andrew Jackson. Van Buren organized the campaign against incumbent President John Adams and put together a coalition that swept Andrew Jackson to the presidency in 1828. Van Buren won the governorship of New York in the same year but resigned just two months after taking office to accept the position of Secretary of State in Jackson's first Cabinet.

Van Buren had enormous respect for President Jackson and became the leading propagandist for the principles of Jacksonian Democracy. The ideal of equal opportunity for the common man against the forces of vested interest proved a powerful political force and swept Jackson to a stunning second victory in 1832. Shrewd political maneuvering on Van Buren's behalf soon saw him replace Vice-President John Calhoun as Jackson's successor-in-waiting.

Presidential record

Van Buren is often unfairly portrayed as a political opportunist who had no genuine beliefs of his own who rode to the presidency on the poularity of Andrew Jackson. Although it is certainly true that Jackson's status gave Van Buren a tremendous boost, Van Buren's record in office demonstrates that he was willing and capable of defending his political beliefs in the face of adversity.

In the election of 1836, Van Buren faced the newly formed Whig Party. His victory was convincing despite the Whig strategy of splitting the vote by fielding several candidates. In office, Van Buren sought to continue Jackson's policies to the extent of retaining almost exactly the same cabinet.

Events soon conspired to defeat Van Buren's plans. The first great economic crisis in US history, the Panic of 1837, hit the nation hard and came to dominate Van Buren's term. He resisted Whig calls for direct aid to the business community even when Democrats began to defect to the Whigs. Pushing for a Federal treasury independent of the commercial banking system, Van Buren eventually got his wish at the cost of a great deal of political support.

As the election of 1840 approached, the Democrats were crippled by factional disputes and defections. In contrast, the Whigs ran a well-organized and clever campaign that won their nominee, William Henry Harrison, the presidency.

Retirement
Van Buren left the White House at the age of 58, his political career far from over. He narrowly missed the Democratic nomination in 1844 because of his

opposition to the annexation of the then independent state of Texas.

Growing tensions over the issue of slavery produced a split in the Democratic Party. Van Buren headed a faction of the party that was demanding the non-extension of slavery to the new Mexican territories. This faction held their own convention and nominated a reluctant Van Buren as their presidential candidate for the 1848 election. The "Free Soil" bid for the presidency was unsuccessful but did ensure a Whig victory.

After spending several years traveling in Europe, Van Buren retired to his Kinderhook home where he died in July 1862, at the age of 79.

Franklin Pierce

1804–1869
14th President of the US (1853–57)
Democrat

Notable dates

Nov 23, 1804	*Birth*
1834	*Married Jane Means Appleton*
Nov 2, 1852	*Elected President*
Mar 4, 1857	*Retired from presidency*
Oct 8, 1869	*Death*

Background

Born in Hillsborough, New Hampshire, Franklin Pierce was the son of the future Governor of that state. He was educated at Bowdoin College, from which he graduated in 1824, and then studied law gaining admittance to the New Hampshire Bar in 1827.

At the age of only 25, Pierce began his political career with election to the New Hampshire legislature. Just three years later he was elected to Congress and only four years after that became a Senator. Although he rarely spoke on the floor, he was a commited Jacksonian and worked hard on committees.

In 1834, Pierce married Jane Means Appleton, an aristocratic Whig. The union proved difficult for Pierce since his wife was a fanatical member of the temperance movement. She was appalled by the amount of drinking that went on in political circles and persuaded her husband to resign from the Senate and move away from Washington.

Still active in local politics for the Democrats, he impressed President James Polk so much that he was appointed Federal District Attorney of New

Hampshire in 1845. Pierce turned down an invitation to join the Cabinet in 1846 and instead enlisted in the Army as a private to see action in the Mexican War.

By the end of the war Pierce was a Brigadier-General. He returned home in 1848 and threw himself into politics again. He received the Democratic Party presidential nomination in 1852 and was duly elected President in the election of that year with a significant majority over his Whig opponent. At 48, he was the youngest President in history.

Presidential record

Pierce was immensely likeable and affable man who made friends easily and was eager to please. Once in office, he quickly discovered that the promises he had made to gain support were not going to be easy to carry out. It was a time of great tension in the United States as the national debate over slavery was raging, and would eventually lead to the Civil War.

Pierce lacked the vision and skills to tackle the tremendous difficulties of the period – perhaps any man would have. He was also distracted by personal tragedy. In 1853, the Pierce family were in a train wreck in which their only surviving child, 11-year-old Benjamin, was killed. Mrs Pierce, already unhappy at returning to Washington, withdrew completely from public life from this time on.

The slave issue blew up in 1854 with the introduction of the Kansas-Nebraska bill which was to allow settlers in those two new states to decide for themselves whether slavery should be legal there. Pressure from senators forced Pierce to endorse the bill, even though he foresaw the difficulties it was going to cause. Proslavery and antislavery activists rushed to the new territories and promptly started a local civil war. Pierce sent in troops to quell the disorder but failed to stamp out the problem.

In foreign policy, Pierce was very active although he achieved little. Perhaps the most significant moment came when US Navy warships sailed to Japan in order to open up trade and diplomatic relations with that nation. Japanese shock as they first encountered the western military technology brought about a kind of revolution in Japan that was to lead ultimately to Pearl Harbor.

Attempts to win Cuban independence from Spain came to nothing and a rash action in Nicaragua almost brought war with Britain. With the slave issue spinning out of control, Pierce was unelectable and did not stand for nomination for a second term.

In retirement, Pierce vehemently attacked President Lincoln for his conduct of the Civil War. He died in Concord, a virtual recluse, at the age of 64.

James Buchanan

1791–1868
15th President of the US (1857–1861)
Democrat

Notable dates

Apr 23, 1791	*Birth*
1845–48	*Secretary of State*
Nov 4, 1856	*Elected President*
Mar 4, 1861	*Retired from presidency*
1861–65	*American Civil War*
June 1, 1868	*Death*

Background

Born near Mercersberg, Pennsylvania, James Buchanan grew up on the frontier trading post owned by his father. He attended Dickinson College, graduating with honors in 1809, and then studied law. After admission to the Bar in 1813, he established a legal practice in Lancaster, Pennsylvania.

In 1819, Buchanan became engaged to Ann Caroline Coleman, the daughter of a wealthy industrialist. Family disapproval of the match and unfounded gossip caused Ann to break off the engagement and, a week later, she died, a possible suicide. Buchanan never married after this incident and became the only bachelor President.

The following year, despite receiving blame for the tragedy, Buchanan was elected to Congress. He was to serve five terms from 1821 to 1831. This period saw the death of Buchanan's Federalist Party and the rise of Andrew Jackson. Although Buchanan and Jackson fell out, Buchanan's politics remained Jacksonian.

When Jackson won the presidency in 1828, he appointed Buchanan minister to Russia and Buchanan was able to negotiate the first commercial treaty between the two nations. From 1834 to 1845, Buchanan served in the Senate. Under President James Polk, he was Secretary of State and managed to prevent war with Britain over the Oregon territories.

During the troubled presidency of Franklin Pierce, Buchanan was minister to Britain and became reluctantly involved in Pierce's disastrous attempt "to detach" Cuba from Spain. With Pierce soon out of office, Buchanan received the Democratic nomination in 1856.

Presidential record

No President in the history of the United States has been more unfairly represented than James Buchanan. His presidency came at a time of national near-hysteria over the slave issue that was to result in the devastating Civil War. Despite claims to the contrary made by the Republican victors of the war, Buchanan did everything he could to prevent war and indeed kept the lid on the rising tensions throughout his difficult term. It is unlikely that any man in Buchanan's position could have prevented the looming national tragedy.

A state of civil war had come into existence during

President Pierce's term in the new territories of Kansas. The Kansas-Nebraska bill of 1854 had allowed settlers in the new territories to decide for themselves whether slavery should be legal there or not. When the time came to vote, the antislavery majority refused to register to vote. Consequently, the proslavery lobby won the day which only raised tensions further.

Buchanan adopted the English bill which cleverly put off the decision as to whether to admit Kansas to the Union until 1861, when it was admitted as a free state. The key had been to promise Kansas more land if it waited for admission. This bought Buchanan time and allowed the situation to calm down. Unfortunately, it was widely regarded as a Southern swindle in the North and added to Buchanan's unpopularity there.

Buchanan's personal view was that slavery should be ended throughout the Union, but his political morals prevented him from saying so. Throughout his long period in public service – 40 years before becoming President – he had been guided by the principles that citizens must obey the law even if they thought it unjust and that moral issues should not be decided by politics. For Buchanan, the fact that slavery was legal in the Southern states meant that he was bound to defend it until such time as the law was changed.

Buchanan did not stand for nomination in 1860 and the Democratic Party was disastrously split between North and South — Abraham Lincoln's victory was inevitable. Once the war began, Buchanan strongly supported the Union but gradually he came to be regarded as a scapegoat and withdrew completely from public life.

Buchanan lived to see the Union victory, and the assassination of its chief architect, Abraham Lincoln. He died at his home in June 1868. Only recently have historians begun to reassess the career of this much maligned man.

Benjamin Harrison

1833–1901
23rd President of the US (1889–1893)
Republican

Notable dates

Aug 20, 1833	*Birth*
1853	*Married Caroline Scott*
1881–87	*Senator*
Nov 4, 1888	*Elected President*
Mar 4, 1893	*Retired from presidency*
Mar 13, 1901	*Death*

Background

Born at North Bend, Ohio, into a wealthy and long established land-owning family, Benjamin Harrison was the grandson of President William Henry Harrison, 9th President of the US. At age 14, he went to Cary's College and in 1850 moved to Miami University in Oxford, Ohio. Graduating in 1851, he toyed with the idea of becoming a minister in the Presbyterian Church but settled on law.

1853 brought marriage to Caroline Scott, whom he had met at college. Shortly after this his father, John Scott Harrison, was elected to Congress and left the running of the family estate at North Bend in Benjamin's hands. The following year, Harrison was admitted to the Bar and moved to Indianapolis, where he eventually formed a successful partnership with William Wallace.

Harrison's father warned him to stay away from politics but Harrison campaigned for the Republican presidential candidate in 1856 – breaking with his father's Whig politics. His legal career was progressing satisfactorily when the Civil War intervened. Asked by the Governor of Indiana to form the 70th Indiana Regiment, Harrison put together and drilled a body of men that were to win fame for their valor in the coming conflict. Harrison himself served bravely and, in recognition, was given the rank of Brigadier-General.

Harrison was a war hero when he returned to Indianapolis to continue his legal career. He ran unsuccessfully for the governorship of Indiana but, by 1888, had risen to such prominence in the Republican Party that he received the nomination to run against President Cleveland. The election was close, with Harrison receiving less of the popular vote than Cleveland but winning the important states of Indiana and New York to clinch victory.

Presidential record

Harrison is an underrated President today, but his administration built solidly on the foundations it inherited and helped to create a United States that was ready to take on the responsibilities and difficulties of its emerging superpower status. Inaugurated 100 years after George Washington, he is often known as the "Centennial President."

Promising a "legal deal" during his campaign, Harrison set about tackling long-standing economic and social problems. With a Republican majority in Congress, Harrison was able to enact most of his legislative program before 1891. The Sherman Antitrust Act outlawed monopolies that were interfering with small businesses and farmers. The McKinley Tariff Act set tariffs at record levels to protect American industry during a period of rapid but fragile industrialization. The Dependent Pension Act gave greater help to Civil War veterans who could not perform manual work.

In foreign policy, Harrison's policies were again sure, steady, and far-sighted. He initiated the building of a two-ocean navy and organized the first Pan American Conference in 1889 which opened the way for increased trade with Latin America. Serious diplomatic incidents which could have brought conflict with Italy and Chile were handled deftly and war with Britain and Germany over control of Samoa was avoided. His one regret was his failure to secure Hawaii as a US territory.

Harrison stood for and won the Republican nomination in 1892 and once again faced the re-nominated Cleveland. When the Populist candidate James Weaver entered the fight, a significant proportion of Harrison's support was siphoned off.

There was also discontent over the McKinley Tarriff. In a lacklustre campaign during which Harrison's wife died, he lost out to Cleveland and retired to Indianapolis.

Retirement

Aged 59, at his retirement from the presidency, Harrison returned to his legal practice and made it into a great success. In 1896, he married Mary Lord Dimmock, his first wife's niece and, the following year, published *This Country of Ours*, a guide to the operation of the Federal government. He died in Indianapolis in March 1901.

William Howard Taft

1857–1930
27th president of the US (1909–13)
Republican

Notable dates

Sep 15, 1857	*Birth*
1886	*Married Helen Herron*
Nov 3, 1908	*Elected President*
Mar 4, 1913	*Retired from presidency*
1921–30	*Chief Justice of the US*
Mar 8, 1930	*Death*

Background

Willliam Howard Taft was born in Cincinnati, Ohio. His father was a lawyer who later became Secretary of War and Attorney General under President Ulysses S Grant. Graduating with distinction from Yale in 1878, Taft attended the Cincinnati Law School and was admitted to the Bar in 1880. The law was to be Taft's passion throughout his life.

Helen Herron, whom Taft married in 1886, was to have a major influence on his life. It was she who persuaded him to enter politics, an arena he had little taste for. By 1890, Taft was appointed Solicitor General by President Benjamin Harrison.

A great opportunity came for Taft in 1900 when he was appointed head of a commission to bring self-rule to the Phillipines. The islands had become a US possession after victory in the Spanish-American War and it had always been a US aim to make them self-governing. In contrast to the US military's rule of the islands, Taft's governorship was marked by tolerance and a real desire to improve the lives of the islanders.

In 1901, Theodore Roosevelt became President after the assassination of McKinley. Roosevelt and Taft were firm friends although of very different character. Roosevelt was convinced that Taft should be his successor and persuaded him to return to the US and take on the post of Secretary of War. Although reluctant to leave his work in the Phillipines, Taft accepted. "Politics, when I am in it, makes me sick" he later wrote to his wife – yet in 1908, he accepted the Republican presidential nomination. Her ambition and the insistence of Roosevelt had been major factors in the decision.

Presidential record

Taft's reluctance to become President proved to be well-founded. Although a thoroughly able and honest man, a combination of bad luck and a lack of vision meant that his term in office was disastrous.

Among his few achievements were the establishment of the parcel post and the creation of a separate Department of Labor. Also during his term Arizona and New Mexico, the last of the 48 contiguous states, joined the Union. He continued the battle against trusts (business monopolies) begun by Roosevelt but received little credit for it. Attempts to increase trade through a free-trade agreement with Canada also came to nothing.

Political infighting in Congress proved to be Taft's undoing. When the Democrats gained control of the House in 1910, Progressive Republicans looked to former President Roosevelt as their leader. When the time came for presidential candidate nomination in 1912, Roosevelt actually stood against his old friend and ally Taft. Although Taft secured the nomination, Roosevelt decided to stand against him as an independent candidate. With the Republican Party in chaos, Taft was virtually unelectable and he came third in the election. The Democratic candidate Woodrow Wilson strode to victory.

Later life

Disheartend by his experiences of national politics, Taft became a law professor at Yale. During World War I, he served as chairman of the National War Labor Board and came into close contact with organized labor groups for the first time.

In 1921, Taft had the opportunity to fulfil his genuine lifetime ambition. With the death of the incumbent Chief Justice, Taft won the appointment to head the Supreme Court. He became the only person in history to have held that office and the presidency. It was a happy time for Taft and, although not spectacular, his achievements were solid and of lasting good to the nation's system of justice.

Heart disease meant that Taft had to retire from his post in February of 1930. Just over a month later he died in Washington, DC.

Herbert Clark Hoover

1874–1964
31st President of the US (1929–33)
Republican

Notable dates

Aug 10, 1874	*Birth*
1899	*Married Lou Henry*
Nov 6, 1928	*Elected President*
Mar 4, 1933	*Retired from presidency*
Oct 20, 1964	*Death*

Background

Herbert Hoover was born in West Branch, Iowa, into a long-established Quaker family. His father, a blacksmith, died when Hoover was six and his mother also died less than three years later. Sent to live with his uncle in Newberg, Oregon, Hoover attended a Quaker academy and continued his education at night school after he began to work.

At 17, Hoover entered Stanford University and demonstrated great skill in mathematics and geology – he graduated with an engineering degree in 1895. From this point until the very end of his life Hoover applied himself diligently to a bewildering array of jobs and careers. Working as a mining engineer he quickly gained a reputation for excellence and was invited by the Chinese government to head its national mining company.

In 1899, Hoover married Lou Henry and the pair arrived in China just as the Boxer Rebellion began – a violent attempt by some Chinese to eject all foreigners. Hoover and his wife survived the crisis and, during the next three years, his engineering career took Hoover all over the world. By 34, he was wealthy and internationally renowned in his field.

At the outbreak of World War I, Hoover was in

London and was asked by the US Ambassador to direct the evacuation of US citizens stranded in Britain. More relief work in German-occupied Belgium and France to feed some 10 million starving civilians brought him international recognition. When the US entered the war President Woodrow Wilson appointed Hoover US food administrator. He also organized the American Relief Administration which fed and clothed hundreds of millions of Europeans once the war was over.

Hoover's attempt to gain the Republican Party's presidential nomination in 1920 failed but, seven years later when President Calvin Coolidge announced his retirement, Hoover stood again. During this period he had served as Secretary of Commerce and impressed many with his administrative skills. In 1928, he won the nomination overwhelmingly. His victory in the election was even more convincing.

Presidential record

Hoover seemed to be a man destined for the presidency. His excellence as an administrator and his extraodinary contributions to international aid seemed to indicate that he would make an outstanding President. Sadly for Hoover it was not to be. Within months of starting his term in office he was faced with the greatest economic crisis in US history. A massive stock market crash in October 1929 heralded the beginning of the Great Depression – within four years 12 to 14 million Americans were unemployed and many of those were practically starving.

Ironically, after all he had done for the peoples of other stricken countries, there was little Hoover could do for the American people. He opposed the kind of massive Federal spending that Franklin D Roosevelt would later use but did set up a corporation to lend some government money to businesses. It is doubtful that any President faced with the same problems could have radically improved the nation's fortunes during that time. Despite his talents, it proved to be beyond Hoover.

In foreign policy, Hoover was committed to peace and nonintervention. His own experiences had shown him what war could do. Although the US did not join the League of Nations after World War I, Hoover cooperated with its aims and was instrumental in drawing up a treaty to limit naval armaments.

In 1928, Hoover stood for re-election but was soundy defeated by Franklin Delano Roosevelt. The Depression dominated the campaign as it had Hoover's time in office.

Retirement

Although retired from the presidency and now aged 58, Hoover's drive and determination were undiminished. He wrote and campaigned to keep the United States out of World War II and, under President Harry S. Truman, made several international trips to organize relief efforts after the war's end. Truman also appointed Hoover as chairman of the Commission on Organization of the Executive Branch of Government. He finally retired in 1955 at the age of 80 but continued to write. Hoover died, aged 90, in New York City.

James Earl Carter

b.1924–
39th President of the US (1977–81)
Democrat

Notable dates

Oct 1, 1924	*Birth*
1946	*Married Rossalynn Smith*
1971–74	*Governor of Georgia*
Nov 1976	*Elected president*
Jan 20, 1981	*Retired from presidency*

Background

James Earl Carter Jr was born in Plains, Georgia. His father owned a small country store near Plains and farmed. At the age of 9, he was baptized into the First Baptist Church of Plains – an institution that was to have a profound influence on his life. Although he rejected the extreme conservative moralism of his church, he made much of his faith in his later political career.

During World War II, Carter was at the US Naval Academy at Annapolis – he graduated in 1946. Soon after, he married a local Plains girl, Rossalynn Smith. After two years' service on battleships, Carter was accepted for submarine duty and was eventually assigned to the nuclear submarine programme.

When his father died in 1953, Carter resigned from the Navy and returned to Plains to take over the family business. He worked hard and, slowly, success came. The farm expanded and started to earn more and more money under his management. By 1954, he was also chairman of the Sumter County school board.

When the Supreme Court ruled that segregation in public schools was unconstitutional, a period of social upheaval swept across Georgia and the rest of the

South. In Plains, a White Citizen's Council movement was formed, which Carter refused to join. For a while his business was boycotted. He advanced plans to integrate the schools, which were defeated, fuelling his desire to become involved in politics.

After two consecutive terms in the Georgia Senate, Carter sought and won the governorship. During his term he fought hard to reverse racist attitudes and even placed a portrait of Martin Luther King in the state capitol building – an act unthinkable only a few years before.

Presidential record

When Carter stood for nomination as the Democratic presidential candidate he was practically unknown in national politics. His election the following year marked the climax of the most meteoric rise in US political history. The nation was at that time extremely disenchanted with Washington and the Federal government. Watergate and the Vietnam War had drained the office of the President of its credibility. Carter saw that the country was ready for a man who was totally unconnected with these recent traumatic events.

Carter promised to bring decency and honesty to the presidency and the American people were persuaded – just. After a very narrow victory over the incumbent President Gerald Ford, Carter began his term in office in 1977. One of his first acts was to sell the presidential yacht and to eliminate many of the ceremonial trappings of the presidency, a move calculated to show that he was serious about changing things in Washington.

The emphasis of Carter's foreign affairs policy was human rights. His frequent criticism of the Soviet Union's human rights record did not prevent him from reaching an historic arms limitation agreement with Soviet leader Brezhnev. Unfortunately, the SALT II treaty was never ratified by the Senate.

The greatest crisis in Carter's presidency came in November 1979, when radicals seized US embassy staff in Teheran, Iran. More than a year of negotiations with Teheran failed to secure their release and an attempted airborne rescue failed disastrously.

At home Carter had inherited an economy that was slowly emerging from the worst economic slump since the 1930s. Inflation and unemployment were continuing to rise, however, and the general

Background

George Herbert Walker Bush was born in Milton, Massachusetts. His father was a wealthy investment banker and, later, a Republican senator. With his sister and three brothers, Bush grew up in Greenwich, Conneticut. He was raised to work hard and to strive for success — but it was also instilled in him to be a team player, a quality that was to serve him well in his future political career.

World War II interrupted Bush's education. He enlisted in the US Navy at age 18 and, for a while, was the Navy's youngest pilot. The future President flew dozens of combat missions in the Pacific theater and survived being shot down over the ocean.

Returning from active service, Bush married Barbara Rye, with whom he was to have six children. Within three years Bush had graduated Phi Beta Kappa from Yale University. Deciding not to go into his father's firm Bush went into the oil industry. By 42, he was able to sell his share in the Zapata Off-Shore Company for a healthy profit and set his sights on a political career.

After having failed once, Bush won election to the House of Representatives in 1964, the first

Republican to represent Houston. He was re-elected for a second term in 1968. Despite this success he lost his second Senate race in 1970, but was appointed as Permanent Representative to the United Nations by President Nixon.

During the Watergate crisis, Bush defended Nixon until he became convinced that the President had lied. Gerald Ford rewarded this loyalty with an important job leading the US liaison office in China. Bush's time in this job contributed significantly to much improved relations between the two nations. Once again he was given a difficult but rewarding job – the directorship of the CIA.

Between 1976 and 1980, Bush was out of political life. When future President Ronald Reagan selected Bush as his running mate, his political future was secured. Serving under the immensely popular Reagan, his ability to work as part of a team lent a solid foundation to the administration and earned him the respect of the American people.

Presidential record

When Bush secured the Republican nomination in 1988, his success at the election seemed almost inevitable. Although there were questions about his ability to handle politics in the limelight, his unswerving loyalty to Reagan made him a natural successor.

In office Bush's policies were virtually a mirror image of Reagan's. Although he did not have the personal charm of Reagan, he was seen as a safe and trustworthy leader. His long political experience and sharp intelligence meant that, although his administration appeared identical to Reagan's, it was actually more professional, better informed, and better run.

While Bush's foreign policy triumphs earned him considerable support, growing economic problems and stalemate with Congress at home undermined his position. Despite his election promise "Read my lips. No new taxes," the ballooning deficit forced Bush to try and increase taxation. When Congress threw out a deficit reduction plan, with the help of many Republican members, the Federal government was almost forced to shut down for lack of money. An eventual compromise reached with the Democratic leadership was never really forgiven by many in the Republican party.

One of Bush's first significant acts in office was to

order troops into Panama to arrest General Noriega. The dictator was captured, tried, and convicted in a US court. The collapse of Soviet power in Eastern Europe caught Bush and the rest of the world by surprise, but the President handled the situation well and did as much as he could to make sure the transition was a peaceful one.

When Iraq invaded the tiny oil-rich nation of Kuwait in August of 1990, Bush saw that there was little hope of a peaceful solution. Once again his diplomatic skills enabled him to form a strong and well-motivated coalition of nations to liberate Kuwait. A massive air bombardment devastated much of Iraq's armed forces and infrastructure before ground forces rolled in to finish the operation in just 100 hours. US forces formed the bulk of those used in the Gulf War and their success was a massive popularity boost for Bush.

Despite these successes the mood of the nation was changing. The extreme right-wing stance of the Republican Party did not help Bush in the 1992 campaign and the Democratic candidate Bill Clinton defeated him by a significant majority.

Chapter Seven

Now and the future

THE TRULY GREAT American Presidents, as featured in the first chapter of this book, could not have foreseen how the nation would develop in the years beyond their deaths. It is unlikely that Washington, Lincoln, or Jefferson would even recognize the America of the 21st century. What will the new millennium have in store for the presidency? Will the electorate vote in America's first black President? When will we see the first female President?

The current incumbent, George W. Bush, and those who follow him, have the burden of governing the most powerful nation in the world. In terms of history, the first half of the 20th century will be viewed as one of the bloodiest periods the world has ever known. It is the responsibility of the present and future Presidents to ensure that the world never again bears witness to the horrors of a World War, while at the same time protecting the interests of the United States.

New concerns face the new Presidents. The United States' record on the environment remains poor, and all indications point to the fact that the world is on the brink of a crisis. Global warming is now a fact, and the President needs to balance the needs of industry against the increasing effects of pollution.

The President of the United States is now considered to be the most powerful person on the planet. The challenges facing the present and future leaders of the United States are great. Domestic policies have to be weighed up against ever-important foreign policies, as the United States increases its role as a force for peace throughout the world.

George W. Bush

b.1946–
43rd President of the US (2001–)
Republican

Notable dates

July 6, 1946	*Birth*
Nov 5, 1977	*Married Laura Welch*
1994–2000	*Governor of Texas*
Jan 20, 2001	*Presidential oath of office*

Background

George W. Bush was born on July 6, 1946, and grew up in Midland and Houston, Texas. He received a bachelor's degree from Yale University in 1968 and an MBA from Harvard Business School in 1975.

Upon his graduation from Yale, Bush became eligible for the draft. He volunteered for the Texas Air National Guard, which meant that he was not drafted, and effectively avoided combat during the Vietnam War. Bush's motivation for joining the Air National Guard was to become a fighter pilot, and he spent two years in flight training and a further four years in part-time service, flying F-102 planes.

In 1975, he began his career in the oil and gas industries, working in energy until 1986. In 1977, Bush set up "Arbusto Energy," an oil company. Bad luck seemed to be attracted to the business, particularly in the form of ever-falling oil prices, and despite his best efforts, Bush sold the company when it had accrued $3 million in debts.

It seems logical that George W. Bush followed the road into politics. He spent 1986 and 1987 working on his father's Presidential campaign, moving to Washington in 1987 to devote himself to the task full-time. Following on from the success of this campaign, he returned to Texas, where he attracted a group of investors to buy the Texas Rangers baseball team.

Being part owner of the Rangers raised Bush's profile in Texas, and, in 1993, he decided to run for Governor. He was elected Governor of Texas on November 8, 1994, beating Democrat Governor Ann Richards.

Bush was re-elected as Governor of Texas on November 3, 1998, becoming the first Texas Governor to be elected to consecutive four-year terms. During his office, he delivered the two largest tax cuts in state history to Texas taxpayers, worth nearly $3 billion.

Presidential campaign

The 2000 campaign for President proved to be one of the closest in electoral history, and the result remains controversial. America went to the polls on November 7, 2000, and it soon became apparent that Democrat candidate Al Gore and Republican candidate George W. Bush were going to run right to the wire for the presidency.

Florida soon became the most important state – the election was so close that whoever won Florida would win sufficient electoral votes to become President. Bush was announced the winner of Florida by just 1,725 votes – close enough to trigger an automatic recount. It soon developed that there was also something wrong with some of the ballot papers, resulting in 19,000 votes being disqualified. This sparked a series of court cases, with both parties seeking crucial recounts.

The issue was finally decided on December 12, 2000, when the US Supreme Court halted recounts of disputed Florida ballots, in effect ruling in Bush's favor. Unofficial recounts as late as January 29, 2001 indicate that Gore may have won Florida had the recounts been allowed to continue by the Supreme Court.

Bush was elected with a minority of the popular vote – Gore polled more than half a million votes in excess of him. Regardless of the controversies, George W. Bush is the 43rd President of the US, and takes his place in the history books as only the second President whose father had also been President.

Policies

Bush has proposed several bold initiatives, including sharp tax reductions, a strengthening of the military, and social security and Medicare reforms. He plans to develop the Strategic Defense Initiative (the "Star Wars" program, initiated under Reagan's presidency) to protect America from possible rogue nations.

His biggest commitment is to education, where he hopes to improve public schools by strengthening local control and ensuring that states are accountable for results. Parents will have access to annual performance figures, and therefore have a more informed choice about their children's education.